Mothers-In-Law
Do Everything Wrong

Mothers-In-Law Do Everything Wrong

Liz Bluper and Renée Plastique

Note: Names have been changed to protect the guilty

Illustrations by Sharon J. Glassman

**Andrews McMeel
Publishing**

Kansas City

Illustrations © 2004 by Sharon J. Glassman

04 05 06 07 08 MLT 10 9 8 7 6 5 4 3 2 1

Library of Congress Control Number: 2003065067

ISBN: 0-7407-4208-6

Book design/composition: Kelly & Company, Lee's Summit, Missouri

With infinite love to our fabulous husbands,
Lloyd and Paul. Although we hate to admit it,
without our mothers-in-law we wouldn't have you.

And to our wonderful children—
all of whom were patient beyond belief while
we worked on this book. We love you more
than words can say. May this book prevent
us from becoming what we write.

Contents

Acknowledgments

*W*e'd be remiss if we didn't hand out several very special thank-yous to those who helped us realize our dream of spreading MILDEW. No, no. Scratch that. Let's try that again. Our dream is to share MILDEW . . . Nope. Wrong again. Our dream . . . okay, here it is . . . We'd like to thank those who helped us realize our dream of lending support to our fellow MILDEW sufferers—you know, those who are experiencing or have experienced an all-too-familiar phenomenon . . . "mother-in-law problems."

The enormity of the Internet—the ability to reach so far so easily—really hit us when we were collecting stories for this book. But our reach would have missed the mark more often than not without the invaluable network and tremendous generosity of WorldWIT: Women in Technology. The women of WorldWIT are some of the brightest, funniest, and most generous you could ever hope to meet. They and many other wonderful, generous women and men from all over the world helped to make this book what it is . . . darn funny. We couldn't have done it without you!

An extra-special "with whipped cream on top" thank-you goes to author extraordinaire Amy Krouse Rosenthal. With her superhuman powers Amy single-handedly put us in touch with those who could make our dream a reality (she also leaps tall buildings in a single bound).

Of course, we also owe a special thank-you to our book's illustrator, Sharon Glassman. Her humorous and creative drawings make our stories come alive with their whimsy, cleverness, and artistry. Sharon, you succeeded beyond our expectations.

And we certainly couldn't live with ourselves unless we shared our deepest gratitude with the brave souls at Andrews McMeel Publishing. They have been kind beyond words. Stephanie Bennett, our calm, cool, and collected editor, has been unerringly supportive, patient, and an all-around good sport. We really like that she laughs at our jokes, too. Stephanie, without you and your colleagues, we couldn't have realized our ten-year-old dream. So without further ado, "Thank you!"

*Mothers-In-Law
Do Everything Wrong*

CHAPTER ONE

What Is MILDEW?
Where Did It Come From?

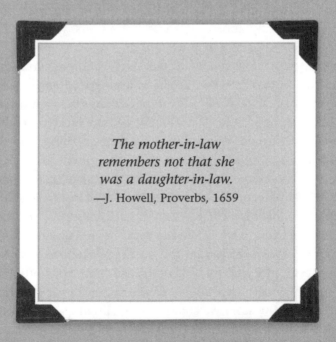

*The mother-in-law
remembers not that she
was a daughter-in-law.*
—J. Howell, Proverbs, 1659

$\mathcal{D}$o you keep hoping that aliens will kidnap your mother-in-law? If so, you must have MILDEW. It's an acronym for Mothers-In-Law Do Everything Wrong, and was created out of necessity. In our experience, it typically refers to a husband's mother, although it occasionally applies to wives' mothers, too.

MILDEW was created when the two of us found ourselves on the phone frequently discussing challenging situations involving our mothers-in-law. Realizing that our husbands would not fully appreciate these discussions, we needed a secret code; thus, MILDEW was born!

Suddenly, we were able to talk freely. Our conversations changed from secretive whispers to relaxed exchanges. All it took was a change from, "My mother-in-law said the most incredible thing . . ." to "My MILDEW said the most incredible thing . . ." Our husbands never suspected a thing, and we were able to commiserate with each other undetected.

In fact, there was a time when Renée called Liz for some MILDEW advice, only to reach Liz's answering machine. Renée left the following message: "Liz, I've got a MILDEW problem and I need your advice. Call me back." As it happened, Liz's husband, Lloyd, picked up the message. When he gave Liz the message he said, "Hey, Renée called. She's got a problem cleaning her bathroom and needs you to call her back." When Liz relayed the story we couldn't stop laughing—it worked! But is that what husbands think their wives talk about?

The more we told our friends about MILDEW, the more we heard funny and outrageous stories. An informal group developed over time, and we found that sharing stories lent much-needed support and added humor to our own situations. We've come to feel that it is our duty to wifedom to share our stories and strategies with wives-at-large.

We realize that some husbands have MILDEW, too. However, husbands seem more reluctant to seek support or share their experiences (unless it relates to a ruined or missed sporting event).

It may surprise you to know that the origins of the MILDEW condition, heretofore identified only as "mother-in-law problems," go back centuries and can be found in numerous historical literary references. The earliest mention we found dates back to ancient Rome. The writer Juvenal, who satirized many facets of Roman life during the first and second centuries A.D., wrote the following: "Give up all hope of peace so long as your mother-in-law is alive." Okay, so that sounds a bit harsh. But if you've had an especially difficult bout of MILDEW, it *is* kind of funny. More to the point, though, MILDEW transcends time and place. Now it's time to wipe that MILDEW away!

It is important to note that not all mothers-in-law are MILDEWs. There are many women and men who can't say enough wonderful things about their mothers-in-law—and we should know; we heard and read many of their stories. In fact, sometimes we got a little jealous.

To help women determine whether they *have* MILDEW or *are* MILDEW, we have developed a highly scientific, delicately calibrated quiz. You'll find the quiz in Chapter 2.

In the meantime, we hope that when our time comes, we will have learned our lessons well and not become MILDEWs ourselves.

NOTE: We wrote this book under pseudonyms in order to protect the guilty. We don't want to cause *too* much trouble with our husbands. All story attributions are also under pseudonyms—we don't want wives or husbands getting into trouble with their mothers-in-law!

———∽∽∽———

CHAPTER TWO

MILDEW Buildup

*However much you dislike your
mother-in-law you must not
set fire to her.*
—Ernest Wild (Recorder of London)
to a culprit before him, c. 1925

*The husband's mother
is the wife's devil.*
—German Proverb

*If I had my way, I am afraid I would
abolish mothers-in-law entirely.*
—Sir Geoffrey Wrangham

*D*o you have MILDEW? The first step in eradicating MILDEW is confirming that you do, in fact, have MILDEW buildup. Detection can be tricky. Oftentimes, it grows slowly—an incident here, a contributing factor there. According to Germany's environmental protection agency, MILDEW is harmful to your health and may trigger allergies and inflammation. Are you inflamed after a visit from MILDEW? You may be allergic to her. According to both an online wool bedding store and several industry and governmental sources:

> If you suspect a MILDEW problem, it's probably true. MILDEW is quite common. Identification is the most important step. A MILDEW problem in the home needs to be followed to its source in order to effectively eradicate it. If left untreated, it may spread.

Answering the simple questions that follow will help you detect MILDEW. It is important to note that detection is the first critical step in combating a MILDEW problem. If you answer "yes" to ten questions, you have MILDEW buildup. If you answer "yes" to twenty-five or more, you have a chronic MILDEW problem and immediate emergency treatment is suggested. For strategies that may inhibit the spread of MILDEW, see Chapter 5.

YES	NO	*Does your mother-in-law . . .*

❏ ❏ 1. still buy your husband underwear?

❏ ❏ 2. show up at your home unannounced?

❏ ❏ 3. still carry baby pictures of your husband in her purse?

❏ ❏ 4. carry pictures of your husband's ex-girlfriend in her purse?

❏ ❏ 5. call you by the wrong name (typically an ex-girlfriend she liked better)?

❏ ❏ 6. have separate twin beds for you and your husband to sleep in when you visit (à la Rob and Laura Petrie)?

THE TELEPHONE LINE

YES	NO	*Does your mother-in-law . . .*

❏ ❏   7. call every day?

❏ ❏   8. call repeatedly
before you get up
in the morning
or after you go to bed at night?

❏ ❏   9. call when you and your husband are
getting "intimate"?

❏ ❏   10. leave long messages for your husband
on your answering machine—with the
message being a complaint about you?

❏ ❏   11. always call at dinnertime, saying "I know
it's a bad time, but . . ." (while the kids are
screaming in the background)?

❏ ❏   12. (when making her daily call) pretend she
only called to talk to her grandchild—
even though the child cannot speak yet?

❏ ❏   13. keep calling (weekly) to see if you need her
to baby-sit, even though you have *never*
taken her up on her offer?

NO KNOWS

YES	NO	*Does your mother-in-law . . .*
☐	☐	14. dispense unwanted advice?
☐	☐	15. want to know every detail of your life on a daily basis?
☐	☐	16. start many of her sentences with, "I know it's none of my business, but . . ."
☐	☐	17. tell friends and strangers intimate details of your life?

IT'S ALL RELATIVE

YES	NO	*Does your mother-in-law . . .*
☐	☐	18. tell you when to call or visit relatives?
☐	☐	19. invite unwanted relatives to your house?
☐	☐	20. get angry or upset when you spend a holiday with *your* family?
☐	☐	21. tell everyone that your child looks just like relatives from only her side of the family? and that every wonderful trait your child has comes from her side, too?

FOOD FETISH

YES	NO	*Does your mother-in-law . . .*

❏ ❏ 22. insist on giving you groceries and leftovers from her refrigerator?

❏ ❏ 23. cook or bake for you (really for her son), even when you've asked her not to?

❏ ❏ 24. give you her baked goods (or other food she has made) in battered old cereal boxes and cottage cheese containers?

COMING HOME

YES	NO	*Does your mother-in-law . . .*

☐ ☐   25. point out places in your house where cleaning was missed?

☐ ☐   26. make negative comments about how thin your husband looks (referring to your cooking skills)?

☐ ☐   27. make negative comments about your husband putting on weight (again, referring to your cooking skills)?

☐ ☐   28. move around the furniture or knickknacks in your home?

BEST BUY

YES   NO   *Does your mother-in-law . . .*

❏   ❏   29. buy you gifts that she likes but are clearly not your taste?

❏   ❏   30. leave the price tags on gifts she buys you, so you know how much she spent?

❏   ❏   31. give you nonreturnable gifts that she received free or at a deep discount?

❏   ❏   32. repeatedly ask if you've sent thank-you notes to her friends?

DENIAL

YES	NO	*Does your mother-in-law . . .*

❑ ❑ 33. ask you the same question repeatedly when the answer is not the one she wants to hear?

❑ ❑ 34. (relates to #33) When you consistently give that undesired answer, does she ignore you anyway?

❑ ❑ 35. embarrass you in public places, especially in stores and restaurants?

❑ ❑ 36. just plain old drive you crazy? just by her very existence?

DULUTH

CRAZY... 20FT

ST. LOUIS

PITTSBURGH

CHILD'S PLAY
(skip to Question #47 if you do not have children)

YES	NO	*Does your mother-in-law . . .*

YES	NO	
❑	❑	37. play nonsensical games with your kids that drive them (and you) crazy?
❑	❑	38. tell you about wonderful things your children have done—even though you've been in the same room and have seen the same things the whole time?
❑	❑	39. tell you things about your kids that she thinks only *she* knows, even though she sees them a few times a year and you see them every day?
❑	❑	40. treat your children as if they are younger than they really are? and use baby talk?
❑	❑	41. buy your children clothes that are ugly and embarrassing (but you have to make the kids wear them whenever she comes over)?
❑	❑	42. buy your children gifts that you *specifically* asked her not to buy?

❏ ❏ 43. give your children food you specifically told her not to give?

❏ ❏ 44. make negative comments about your children's behavior, referring to your parenting skills?

❏ ❏ 45. let you know that the way you are raising your children is not the way she raised her son and, since her son is perfect, you are obviously doing something wrong?

❏ ❏ 46. after baby-sitting your child, start many of her sentences with, "I know you told me not to, but . . ."

Still unsure whether you have MILDEW buildup?

YES	NO	*You know you have MILDEW if . . .*
❏	❏	47. you break into a cold sweat when you watch episodes of *Everybody Loves Raymond*.
❏	❏	48. you really related to Princess Diana's problems with the Queen.
❏	❏	49. you're watching *Bewitched* and Endora makes you think of MILDEW.
❏	❏	50. you had déjà vu watching *Sex in the City*'s Charlotte and Bunny MacDougal.

__ __ **TOTAL**

Most of us MILDEW sufferers experience it only in our private lives. However, we've discovered that not everyone is so lucky. Before writing this book, it never occurred to us that the "rich and famous" might suffer similar experiences. We have come to realize that no one is immune, regardless of position, social status, or wealth.

As Princess of Wales, Diana experienced the worst kind of MILDEW—Public MILDEW. Her difficult relationship with Queen Elizabeth was regularly dissected in the newspapers and tabloids.

Another Public MILDEW sufferer was Jacqueline Kennedy. When she married Jack Kennedy, Jackie experienced quite a strong case of it. It's difficult to be First Lady when MILDEW has held that position in the family for so many years.

Privately, even Eleanor Roosevelt, one of America's most admired women, was a MILDEW sufferer. Her mother-in-law, Sara, dominated many aspects of Franklin and Eleanor's lives. Eleanor's MILDEW even bought and decorated adjoining New York townhouses for the couple (and herself), as a wedding present no less! This arrangement gave Eleanor's MILDEW free access to the couple's home. After Eleanor and Franklin had several children, MILDEW hired their nannies and told both Eleanor and the children that Eleanor was "only the one who bore you; I am your real mother." Scary!

Just as surprising to us was discovering that the seemingly perfect life of Princess Grace of Monaco was not so perfect. Her marriage to Prince Rainier seemed a fairy tale, but in reality, Princess Grace had to contend with a MILDEW who didn't think she was good enough for her son. Boy, if she wasn't good enough, who is?!

It just goes to show that no one is immune. Even pillars of society—a U.S. president's wife and several princesses—have had MILDEW. These women came from privileged backgrounds and had social status and wealth at their disposal. Even so, they could not avoid MILDEW. Ah, what a woman does for love . . .

CHAPTER THREE

Early MILDEW Indicators

> *Be civil to a mother-in-law*
> *and she will come to your*
> *house three times a day.*
> —Japanese Proverb
>
> *Only Adam had no mother-in-law.*
> *That's how we know he lived*
> *in paradise.*
> —Old Yiddish Saying

There Is a Fungus Among Us . . .

Are you experiencing MILDEW symptoms? Not sure? Below are several cautionary tales that may help you identify a MILDEW problem of your own.

The stage play *Once Upon a Mattress* perfectly illustrates a series of early MILDEW indicators. The play was first performed in New York City in 1959, with Carol Burnett playing the part of Princess Winnifred. The story is based on *The Princess and the Pea,* a popular children's fairy tale by Hans Christian Andersen. For educational purposes, we have highlighted seven MILDEW moments. Think of them as teachable moments, i.e., notable examples of MILDEWness. These moments can be analyzed and discussed with veteran MILDEW sufferers in order to gain a fuller, more complete understanding of the phenomenon—the better to avoid it.

Once Upon a Mattress offers several excellent and, dare we say, typical MILDEW moments. In the synopsis that follows, used courtesy of Decca Broadway, we highlight those moments. Following the synopsis we address the finer points of those moments.

Once Upon a MILDEW?

The story of *Once Upon a Mattress* follows the lives of several characters: (1) the unmarried Prince Dauntless the Drab, (2) his talkative, overbearing mother, Queen Aggravain, who dominates the kingdom, and (3) King Sextimus, the Queen's mute husband, who is under a mysterious spell.

The Prince's mother wants to keep her son all to herself **[MILDEW Moment #1]***, so she has declared that the Prince will wed only a true princess of royal blood. As such, Queen Aggravain insists that any bridal candidate must pass a test of the Queen's own choosing—a dozen girls have already been tested and rejected. **[MILDEW Moment #2]**

Although eager, sometimes the prince has the feeling that the Queen doesn't want him to marry. The Queen accuses him of being ridiculous, trying to explain, "I *want* you to get married, but I don't want you to marry just *anybody* . . . You *are* a prince and you must marry someone suitable, someone who's good enough and smart enough and fine enough for my good, nice, sweet, beautiful baby boy. And of course she has to be a princess. I mean a *real* princess. She has to be a real, genuine, bona fide princess just as I was. That's what you really want, isn't it? Someone like me? Of course you do! Oh, if I were only twenty years younger . . ." **[MILDEW Moment #3]**

At this point, a knight offers to embark on a search for a princess. Reluctant to accept the offer, the Queen finally gives

---

*See p. 24 for MILDEW Moment explanations.

in to Prince Dauntless's pleading and grants permission for the search. Three weeks later, a princess is found—Princess Winnifred. It is at this point that the Queen decides to devise a clever test to determine whether this self-proclaimed princess is worthy of her son.

Hmmmmmm . . . What to test her for . . . Ah ha! A test for *sensitivity.* That might work. But how? The Queen decides to place one tiny pea under twenty soft, downy mattresses. "Any genuine princess would feel it." But the Queen worries that her test may be too easy. So to stack the deck in her favor she also uses a sleeping potion, a hypnotic mirror, and a magic nightingale to sing a lullaby to the Princess. But wait! "The most important thing is that she's tired out first. We'll have an official ball tonight.

We can do that new dance—the Spanish Panic—it's absolutely exhausting." **[MILDEW Moment #4]**

Meanwhile, Winnifred has impressed not only Dauntless, but the King, who, she learns, is under a curse. According to the curse, he will remain mute until "the mouse devours the hawk," whatever that means—no one seems to know. **[MILDEW Moment #5]**

Setting up her test, the Queen demands that the castle remain quiet while it is in progress. "We don't want anything to disturb what's-her-name as she sleeps." [**MILDEW Moment #6**] But Winnifred is definitely having trouble getting comfy, even with the lullaby and sleeping potion. She's on top of those twenty downy mattresses, but it's no use. Bring on the sheep! And she begins to count . . .

The next morning the Queen is certain her test has succeeded. How could anyone possibly pass the test? In fact, she's already gloating over her success when Winnifred arrives on the scene . . . still counting sheep! She hasn't slept a wink all night. "That bed ought to be moved down to the torture chamber!" she says.

Dauntless is delighted! Winnifred has passed the test after all, and now they can be married. But the Queen doesn't give in quite so easily and begins haranguing Dauntless about his choice of a wife. [**MILDEW Moment #7**] Dauntless has finally had enough and he shouts at his mother to *shut up!* It's happened at last—the mouse has finally devoured the hawk. The spell is broken, and now it's the Queen who can't speak and the King's voice is back at last!

Winnifred is exhausted; she really needs to get some sleep. But now we see that it wasn't the pea that kept her awake, but the minstrel's lute, helmet, and other spiked and thorny objects that were placed under the mattresses. Winnifred can finally get a good night's sleep, and she duzzzzzz . . .

MILDEW Moments

1. MILDEW is often unwilling to share her son with another woman, especially one who may take on the role of wife.

2. Because of #1, MILDEW can sometimes devise tests in which the woman is set up to fail.

3. MILDEW often believes that her son should marry someone exactly like herself.

4. Diabolical!

5. Symbolic yet important: MILDEW's mute husband. Be wary.

6. Ah, yes, the old "what's-her-name" trick.

7. Self-explanatory.

The tales that follow are of the pre-MILDEW variety. They may help you identify MILDEW early on, allowing you to decide how best to proceed.

Glove Me Tender

This is a pre-MILDEW story, apparently an indication of things to come. . . . The first time I met my MILDEW-to-be, my husband and I had been dating for a year. We were attending an out-of-state college, and it was the first time I had ever been to his home. As soon as I was introduced, his mother ran to a nearby closet and began rummaging around for something. It took her quite a while; I thought it was the strangest thing . . . Suddenly, she reappeared with a pair of women's gloves and asked, "Are these yours, dear? I think you left them here." My now-husband responded unhappily, "Mom, it's the first time she's been here!" Apparently, they belonged to a previous girlfriend.

—Sonja, *New Jersey*

I Spy

Several years ago I met a fellow, Eric, and we started jogging together. After a few weeks (we were not dating at this point, just jogging buddies), I met his mother when he asked her to drop us off at a certain intersection (since she was going shopping in the area).

She asked me an awful lot of questions . . . I felt like I was being interrogated. At the time I didn't know why (I sure do now!), but Eric refused to supply any details about where we were going, other than "to a friend's house."

When she dropped us off, she sat in the car with the engine idling. As we walked up the street to our friend's house the car slooooooooowly crept along behind us. We walked faster. The car followed, making us feel like we were in a cheesy horror film! We cut through some bushes and waited a few minutes, watching her sit there. I know; sounds crazy, huh?

Just when I grabbed my cell phone to dial 911—after all, I barely knew this man and his mother—she finally drove off. Eric didn't explain, and I didn't ask. But three years later I am happily living with this man. To this day I still refuse to give my cell or work phone numbers to his mother.

—Toni, *Massachusetts*

Not *My* Son

My husband Ben and I lived together for four years before we got married. However, MILDEW (or pre-MILDEW) was in complete denial about our living arrangements. Admittedly, there was some guilt on our part in the early days. I am a painter, and back then, whenever MILDEW called Ben, and I answered the phone, I would tell her that I was there painting since his place was so much bigger than mine. One evening, three years into our living together, we joined his parents for dinner. MILDEW asked, "Are you still painting in Ben's apartment?" My father-in-law turned to her and said, "Face it, Alice, they're living together. They have been for years." She looked at her husband, then at me, and firmly stated, "No, they're not. *My* son wouldn't do something like that." We just kept our heads down and ate our dinners.

—Samantha, *New York*

Ancient MILDEW

Roman mythology offers one of the oldest examples of pre-MILDEW: the story of Cupid, his mother Venus, and his future wife, Psyche. Let's meet the cast of characters:

- Cupid, the god of love, was the son of Venus.

- Venus (aka MILDEW), the goddess of love and beauty, was worshiped by most mortal men.

- Psyche was the mortal daughter of a king; she was the smartest and most beautiful girl in the kingdom.

What follows is the actual story of Cupid, Venus, and Psyche, but with a twist—we've retold it from Psyche's point of view.

As I grew up, men from all over the land began coming to admire me. I was young and foolish—I didn't know why I had so many gentlemen callers. More important, I didn't know that my many admirers had stopped worshiping the goddess Venus. Uh oh. It turns out that Venus was *furious* when she realized that men who normally worshiped her, a love goddess, were instead worshipping me, a mere mortal.

I didn't know it at the time, but Venus nagged Cupid until he finally agreed to poison me. But wait, it wasn't just any old poison. Venus had him use a poison to make me fall in love with lowlifes. Gross!

When Cupid came to do Venus's dirty work, he took one look at me, got discombobulated, accidentally scratched himself with one of his *other* arrows and fell in love with me. I fell for him, too. Again, Venus was *furious* with me. But it wasn't *my* fault that Cupid was a klutz!

I didn't know what to do. My mother warned me not to get involved with the son of a love goddess. But it was too late—I was in love. Knowing that Venus was a goddess and could make my life miserable, I went to her to apologize. But instead of accepting my apology, Venus (now officially pre-MILDEW) made me do four impossible tasks.

Cupid, being the nice guy that he was, helped me finish them. But guess what? Venus was *still* furious! Gosh, there was just no pleasing her (doesn't *that* sound familiar)! Finally, Cupid had had enough and went to his grandfather, Jupiter (Venus's father), and asked for his help. Jupiter was incredibly understanding. He made me immortal and married the two of us. MILDEW, I mean Venus, was furious for weeks. But after about a year we gave her something else to focus on—a beautiful granddaughter named Pleasure. Now MILDEW is driving me crazy with all her parenting advice!

—Psyche, *Italy*

CHAPTER FOUR

It Spreads Like ... a Fungus

> "We never make sport of religion, politics, race or mothers. A mother never gets hit with a custard pie. Mothers-in-law—yes. But mothers—never."
> —Mack Sennett (1884–1966),
> American movie director

> "But there, everything has its drawbacks," as the man said when his mother-in-law died and they came down upon him for the funeral expenses.
> —Jerome K. Jerome, *Three Men in a Boat*, ch. 3, 1889

Is It in Your House
or from Your Spouse?

There is a residue that lingers from MILDEW buildup. Even in
cases where MILDEW is no longer a problem,
the residue can make you overly sensitive. What
are we trying to say here? Well, if your mother
were to show up at your home unannounced,
you might be glad, or at least you probably
wouldn't be upset. But if you've had MILDEW,
experiencing just one unannounced visit could
send you to the isolation ward.

So what we're saying is that MILDEW has repercussions.
The sufferer becomes overly sensitive, even irrational, whenever exposed to MILDEW. It may not be fair, it may not make
sense, but there you have it.

What follows are true stories that have been culled from
near and far. We have collected these MILDEW stories from
all over the world—they span generations as well as cultures.
Mother-in-law "issues" are a truly global experience for count-
less women (and some men).

NOTE: Names have been changed to protect the guilty.

Urban Legends Gone Awry

Many MILDEWs like to share their life experiences and perspectives in hopes of helping their daughters-in-law. But the end result is often not what they intend: They spook their daughters-in-law and/or reduce them to giggles. Below are several examples.

Happy and Gay

When I first brought my baby boy home from the hospital, he started to cry in his crib. I ran to get him, but MILDEW screamed at me not to pick him up. She then proceeded to inform me that if you pick up crying baby boys they will become homosexuals.

—Ainsley, *Colorado*

When It Rains, He Pours

Months after our son was born MILDEW asked me, "Does he pee a lot when it rains? It's because he's a *boy*!" What?!

—Nina, *Ohio*

When Lightning Strikes

My MILDEW was a real worrier. She used to keep glasses of water around the apartment in case lightning struck.

—Hillary, Iowa

Walk This Way

When my son was five months old, all he wanted was for me to hold him while he stood on my lap. But MILDEW advised me that he would be bowlegged forever if I didn't stop. I wasn't even sure what bowlegged meant, but still I shared it with my pediatrician—who had a good laugh.

—Kaitlyn, *Massachusetts*

Short-Changed

When my son was a newborn, I dressed him in one of those one-piece outfits with feet. He was kicking and playing and having a generally grand time. Then MILDEW came into the room. She told me that my son's outfit was too tight and it would crush his toes and stunt his growth. I was a new mother, and although I didn't change his outfit right away, I did change it soon thereafter and threw away the outfit. My son, who is now fifteen years old, is six feet tall and his toes are fine. Thank goodness I threw away the outfit!

—Victoria, *U.K. (United Kingdom)*

Preserve Us

MILDEW grew up during the Depression when wealthy people could afford store-bought items, but poorer folk had to make do with homemade. When my daughter was just beginning to eat solid food we decided not to bother with jars of baby food, but to put some of our table food in the blender—saving money and giving her healthier meals (or so we thought). When MILDEW discovered this, she gasped in horror, "But how will the baby get her preservatives?"

—Brooke, *Kansas*

Fever Be Gone

MILDEW strikes again!! My husband
has been really sick with a nasty
virus for the last several days—
high fever, sore throat, and night
sweats. MILDEW suggested that I
put Vicks VapoRub under his arm-
pits to "take away the fever." She
said she did this for her children
when they were small, and that it works . . . (groan).

—Paloma, *New Mexico*

Only Her Hairdresser Knows for Sure

I have to preface my story by explaining that MILDEW is from the "old country." She's very direct and doesn't hesitate to share her views, whether outdated or not.

Whenever MILDEW sees me she very pointedly states (in her thick accent), "You don't have any gray hair." (I'm fifty years old.)

"Well, I have a little," I respond sheepishly.

"If you don't have gray hair, then you are stupid."

Now don't be shocked. In her view, the village idiot has no gray hair because he has no worries and no life experience. So at my age, according to MILDEW, I should have some gray hair by now. Lately, I kid her and respond, "No I don't have gray hair. I'm too stupid." And we laugh. 'Cause what she's really saying is that I'm a woman of substance.

—Lily, *California*

Medicine (Wo)Man

I remember one incident back when MILDEW and I were just getting to know each other. Those were the days when our relationship was—how do I put it?—tense. We were at a stage where MILDEW was just starting to acknowledge my existence. Anyway, I had been ill with a stomach bug, so I hadn't been around very much.

When I finally went with my husband to visit MILDEW, I explained about the bug and then finished by saying that I was feeling much better now. She must not have heard the last bit and quickly produced a suspiciously dusty-looking bottle, saying that it was stomach medicine. I insisted that I felt much better, but she insisted that I must take it. In fact, the more I protested the more insistent MILDEW became.

Several other members of my husband's family were there and they were obviously amused by the situation. I was on the spot and felt that I couldn't resist anymore without being out and out rude—so I took the medicine.

Was it my imagination or was there a look of glee on MILDEW's face when I drank it? Goodness knows what was in that bottle, but it tasted just *awful*! I know this sounds crazy, but in a strange way it was a bit of a bonding moment between us—I can't say that MILDEW became instantly nicer to me, but I think it paved the way.

—Camille, *Australia*

Hair Today, Gone Tomorrow

MILDEW frequently complains that we are not feeding our two-year-old daughter enough. She says, "If Susie ate more, she would have more hair." Huh?

—Maria, *Pennsylvania*

Designing Women

In 2003 the television show *Makeover Mamas* began airing. Its premise? Mothers-in-law who redecorate a room in their grown, married children's home. They get two days and $1,500 to do it, with disagreements mediated by the show's host. Is it a coincidence that the host is a single woman in no hurry to get married? We think not.

It's funny, but some MILDEWs just can't help themselves. They simply *must* do some redecorating for you—or help you with your housekeeping. MILDEWs know that you wouldn't dream of asking them for help because, well, you wouldn't want to impose—would you? The stories that follow demonstrate just how far MILDEW will go for a one-sided episode of *Trading Spaces*.

They'll Never Notice

When my husband and I went skiing one weekend, we had MILDEW come take care of our two-year-old son. We came home to discover that the furniture in our house had been completely rearranged. We couldn't believe it! My father-in-law even had a bad back from moving the couches, tables, and rugs. As soon as MILDEW left we moved the furniture back.

—Heidi, *Washington, D.C.*

Sticky Situation

My husband and I went on vacation and left our keys with MILDEW so that she could water the plants and feed the cat. While we were away she decided that our old refrigerator needed some sprucing up. So when we arrived back home I found that she had stuck contact paper on the outside of it to cover up the scratches. Needless to say, we retrieved our keys *and kept them.*

—Alanna, *Connecticut*

No Win

Whenever we have guests coming, I always make sure to clean the house and straighten up before their arrival. It's no different with MILDEW—in fact, I take extra care before she comes over. I don't think it matters, though. Every time MILDEW invariably comments, "Obviously, your career is more important to you than keeping house." I'm telling you, I can't win.

—Sasha, *Ohio*

Clean as a Whistle

One night, just a few months after being married, my husband and I came home from work only to discover MILDEW—she was in her girdle and on her knees scrubbing our kitchen floor.

—Naomi, *New Jersey*

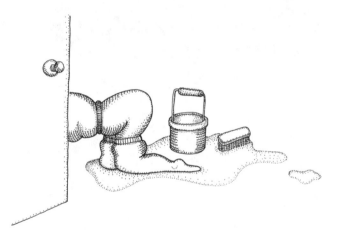

On Trial

A month before my first child was born, MILDEW thought she would help me get our place ready for the baby's arrival. She rearranged our apartment and then went through all of our belongings. I felt like I was on trial for everything I owned as MILDEW continually remarked, "You paid money for this?" By the time she was through I was a basket case!

—Anita, *Iowa*

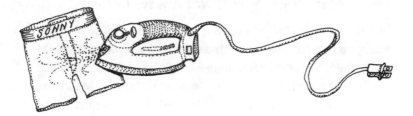

Do Over

When my husband and I relocated back to his old hometown, we moved into MILDEW's home for a few months while we were house hunting. She is lovely, but almost obsessively neat. To keep on good terms we made a special effort to keep our area especially tidy. Apparently, we didn't quite succeed. Each day we would return home from work to find that our bed, which we made before leaving, had been remade. And our clothes, which we had folded and put away in the dresser, had been taken out, ironed, refolded, and put away again—including our underwear! Needless to say, we made sure to find a house *very* quickly.

—Candice, *Georgia*

Less Is More (or Bigger Is Not Always Better)

When my husband and I moved into our first house MILDEW was soon coming around with a stack of do-it-yourself videos on home decoration. She suggested flowered wallpaper for our hallway and velvet drapes instead of blinds. Marching into my bedroom with a gold-framed reproduction of an angelic boy and girl running off into the woods, she said, "Your walls are so empty. This will fit perfectly in here." Before I could say anything, she'd run out to get a rug and baroque candelabra from her car. "For romance," she winked.

Over the next year, my available closet space shrank in direct proportion to MILDEW's surprise gifts. Though her passionate, creative spirit amused me, her insinuations about my lack of style and limited powers of seduction gnawed at me. I became eager to prove myself to her, and transformed our bedroom into a lush garden of love. I even found a place for her candelabra.

"Okaaay," MILDEW droned tentatively when she laid eyes on the cranberry red walls, "Not my color, but I like the silks you've draped around the bed." I thought I'd risen a notch in her eyes, but what came next still shocked me. "Now that you're *my* daughter, too, if you want bigger bosoms, I'll give them to you." Her mischievous eyes met mine as heat rose to my face. Was MILDEW offering me implants? Uncomprehending, I think I mumbled something in response. Then the realization hit: She was trying to redesign me!

—Elle, *Massachusetts*

Cultural Collisions

A lot can get lost in translation. Although the world is turning into one big global community, some customs and beliefs just don't translate. Below, a few transatlantic hiccups.

Hello?

My husband and I have been married now for ten years. MILDEW lives across the country and comes to visit and stay with us pretty regularly. On one such visit, MILDEW and I were watching the evening news together when one of our local reporters, an Asian-American, came on. MILDEW turned to me and said, "I don't know why neither of my sons married an Asian woman. They are so pretty and smart."

—Erica, *New York*

Proper Etiquette

MILDEW is from England, and although she is very nice, she believes that the English have it all over us Americans when it comes to proper etiquette. Well, on one of her visits we were leaving a restaurant when she spied a bowl of mints (with spoon) on the hostess stand. Before we knew what was happening, MILDEW picked up the spoon, retrieved some mints, and put the mints *and* the spoon into her mouth! This is a *very* well-traveled woman, mind you.

—Cecile, *North Carolina*

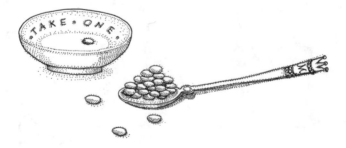

From Russia with Love

I hate to say this, but MILDEW really embarrasses me in public. She lives in Russia, but comes to visit. She's a hefty woman in her fifties. And, well, I don't know how it happened, but somehow she ended up coming with us on our Caribbean vacation. Before the trip I tried explaining that she would need to bring a swimsuit. I offered to take her shopping for one, but she refused. And guess what? The first day we're at the beach MILDEW takes off her clothes and swims in her underwear and tank top. I was *so* embarrassed.

—Emily, *Connecticut*

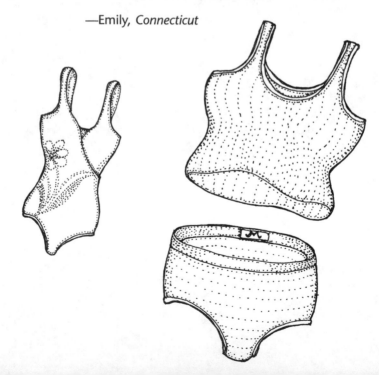

Far and Away

My mother-in-law is great. But maybe that's because I don't get to see her much—she lives in Switzerland.

—Nicole, *Minnesota*

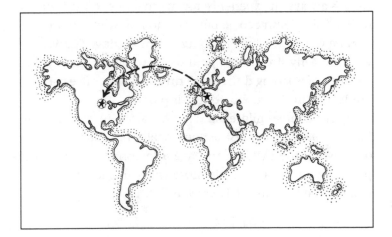

The Help

I admit that I'm very lucky that MILDEW lives Down Under. What's not to like, you ask?

Every other year she comes to visit for a month or two. This is a woman who has "her people" do her housework, cooking, etc. It's always an experience for her to come to the "land of reality." She doesn't cook, but loves to follow me around the kitchen watching what I'm doing and muttering, "Marvelous, you can really stretch that pound of hamburger, can't you?" Her idea of washing dishes is to rinse out her coffee cup and put it back in the cupboard to "drip dry."

We have three children and left her alone to care for them for only *one* day. Clear instructions for all. She thought nothing of allowing the children to have a lemonade stand in the pouring rain (what's a little more water in the lemonade?). Oh, but did I mention? There was lightning.

—Jessica, *Colorado*

Passages from India

Both my husband and I are from India and still have family there. My husband's family, though Indian, now lives in South Africa.

Cultural Confusion

While MILDEW was visiting us from South Africa, we invited my husband's African-American boss to our home. When MILDEW entered the room, she exclaimed, "Oh, you know I am from your native country!" This totally confused the boss, embarrassed my husband, and secretly delighted me.

Maintenance Fee

MILDEW told me that once I start working, I must pay my husband monthly "maintenance" for supporting me.

I Wanna Hold Your Hand

During our trips to the shopping mall and the grocery store my husband and his mother will be holding hands while walking around. Eeeewww!

—Dhara, *Illinois, by way of India*

Here's one MILDEW who's really on top of cultural differences . . .

You Say Po-tay-to and I Say Po-tah-to

When we got engaged, MILDEW threw us an engagement party. To fully appreciate this story you need to know that I am Jewish and my husband is from an old New England Protestant family. At the party, MILDEW was passing around hors d'oeuvres and, not realizing that my family was within earshot, offered the platter to her friends, saying, "Liver pâté?" Then she made an about-face, walked over to us offering, "Chopped liver?" We never said a word about it.

—Carly, *Maine*

Wash 'n' Dry

A Sprinkle a Day

MILDEW lives in the Near East and visits for months at a time. Although she is a wonderful woman, after six months she can drive me a little batty.

Take the bathroom, for instance. In her country, instead of using toilet paper they use a little water hose they have in the bathroom (the idea is similar to a bidet). When MILDEW visits, she refuses to use toilet paper (she says she doesn't feel clean) and instead keeps a gallon water jug in the bathroom. I try to be open-minded, but for some inexplicable reason this habit drives me crazy.

Her last visit was a little different, though. Shortly before her arrival I had bought a slim, modern-looking metal watering can at Ikea. I hadn't decided whether to water my houseplants with it or use it as a planter for my indoor garden. After MILDEW arrived, however, I noticed that it had migrated to the bathroom. Apparently, she had her own ideas on how to use it. I'm not proud to admit this, but I put flowers in the watering can just to annoy her.

Clean or Dirty?

Coming from the Near East, MILDEW doesn't believe in dishwashers. She insists on washing our dishes by hand and then putting them in our dishwasher to drip dry. No amount of explanation or urging can change her mind—apparently, she sees our dishwasher as one big drying rack. It's pretty frustrating when I put in dirty dishes and she puts in clean ones.

—Janet, *California*

Close-Knit

When we first got married, I thought my husband's Eastern European family was going to be an interesting contrast to my American family. But it didn't take long for me to realize that MILDEW sides with only one person in my family . . . her son.

Somehow, we ended up taking the in-laws with us on our honeymoon. We all went together. Yup. One big happy family. As if things weren't bad enough, we had to *share* a hotel room. I tried encouraging MILDEW to take a separate room, but she believes in a family sticking together (apparently no matter what). To top it off, they all snore!

—Bianca, *Illinois*

Happy Holidays?

The holidays can be a stressful time of year—lots of family togetherness. Usually too much togetherness. It doesn't matter which holiday. It doesn't matter which religion. Mixing MILDEW with holidays can be hazardous to your (emotional) health, as demonstrated on the following pages.

Re-Gift

The first time I celebrated MILDEW's birthday with the family (in October) I didn't know what to get her. So I asked my father-in-law. He told me that she had been doing a lot of swimming at the YMCA lately, and needed a bag of some sort for her swimming things. "Aha!" I thought. I bought MILDEW a nice nylon bag with a beautiful, huge, high-quality towel in it. She said that she loved the present. Just a few months later, though, she gave the bag and towel to her grandson for a Christmas present—right in front of me! I looked at her when I realized what had happened, and she said to me, "I got myself some socks with the amount I thought you spent on that present."

—Lauren, *California*

Going Long

I was used to big family Christmas celebrations with lots of laughter and presents to share. At my first Christmas as a wife, and being newly pregnant, I was expecting a similar experience with my new in-laws. As I sat down to enjoy the passing of the presents, I didn't realize that the passing would be literal. MILDEW threw all my presents at me from fifteen feet across the room, even when I wasn't looking! I had to be careful and alert so that I didn't get a black eye.

—Jill, *Missouri*

Brillo Peccadillo

This is a story from one of my closest girlfriends. Every year she has her parents and her in-laws over to her house for Mother's Day dinner. Every year she tries so hard to have everything just right. And every year MILDEW finds some way to completely embarrass  her. The worst? During dinner one year MILDEW said to her, "If you get me some Brillo pads after dinner I'll clean your windows for you."

—Heather, *Washington*

In the Dark

At all our holiday dinners, MILDEW never lights the candles on the table. Not ever. The kids will ask and beg, but she will not light them and we don't know why. She's had the same red tapers for seven years.

—Chloë, *Texas*

Ulterior Motive

One year, MILDEW gave us a set of fine china for a holiday gift. It was a lovely gesture, but one look around our home and you could see that it was not a pattern that fit with our tastes. Soon after, however, I discovered that she had given us the same china pattern as hers so that she could borrow extra pieces when she had company.

—Alice, *Michigan*

Where Have All the Flowers Gone?

It was Rosh Hashanah and MILDEW was coming over for dinner. I spent all day cooking, cleaning, and finally setting the dining room table. I actually went out to my garden to pick and arrange my own flowers and then put the arrangement in the middle of the table. When MILDEW walked in she said, "So, what are you going to use for your centerpiece?"

—Mara, *Washington, D.C.*

Spice Girl

Hosting holiday celebrations requires lots of space to accommodate all our family. Cooking for so many people can be intimidating *and* a lot of work for a new wife. In my experience, most newlyweds start out by going to their parents' or in-laws' homes until they have the space to have everyone to theirs. Not so with my family. On my very first Passover, MILDEW announced that she had just thrown out all her spices, and from now on all holidays were to be celebrated in our six-hundred-square-foot New York City apartment. Not only that, she went on to invite a long list of relatives to our place, too. I guess buying her a spice rack won't change things . . .

—Jordan, *New York*

Eye of the Beholder

At Christmas MILDEW used to buy me sweaters. Always a size small. I am a size large—size fourteen to be exact. Did I actually appear thinner in her eyes?

—Miriam, *Maryland*

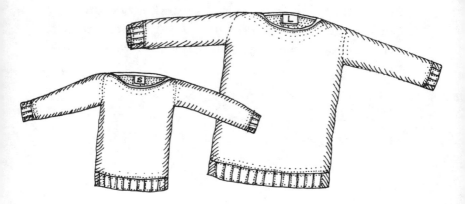

You Shouldn't Have

MILDEW loves to give me "creative" gifts. The problem is, her taste is *completely* different from mine—so much so that it's become downright comical during the holiday season. One year MILDEW gave me a stuffed snowman that dances. When I opened it, I didn't know what to say. The snowman wiggles from side to side while singing "Frosty the Snowman." I just kept saying, "You shouldn't have. No, *really*. You *shouldn't* have."

—Rémy, *New York*

Temptation

MILDEW has a knack for giving *exactly* the wrong gifts to her daughters-in-law. For the daughter-in-law who is on a diet, MILDEW gives industrial-size bags of chocolate from Costco. For the daughter-in-law whose home is decorated in a minimalist, postmodern style MILDEW gives knickknacks and stuffed animals galore. Understandably, the dieting daughter-in-law (my sister-in-law) gets a lot more upset than I do.

—Jocelyn, *Michigan*

Holiday Scene

MILDEW won't come to my home for Christmas anymore because she thinks we don't put up enough decorations! Unless we have every square inch covered in holiday memorabilia MILDEW doesn't think it's festive. Apparently, holiday scenes, complete with moving figures, are a front lawn requirement. I thought the holidays were a time to just appreciate each other . . .

—Vanessa, *Rhode Island*

Company's Coming!

Easter is a really big deal in my husband's family. Every year the family's twenty-five nearest and dearest relatives get together at a local restaurant to celebrate the holiday. A few years ago, MILDEW moved to a new home (the third time in two years, but that's another story). She moved during the first week of February, and that year Easter was the third Sunday of April. Well, one week before Easter MILDEW announced:

1. The restaurant went bankrupt.
2. She had not finished unpacking and it would be impossible for her to host the holiday celebration.

And, best of all:

3. *We* would have to host the holiday celebration.

Aaaaaaaa! Never mind that I had a nine-month-old baby or that our house was best suited for an intimate gathering of, oh, hmmm, let's be generous and say . . . *three*. "Don't worry," said MILDEW, "you won't have to do a thing!" Well, manic shopping, furniture moving, hysterics, and $500 later, my husband's family showed up. Right on cue, the baby began crying and didn't stop through the whole dinner. You know things are bad when you and your husband are fighting over who gets to stay upstairs with the crying baby. Even worse, for a whole year after that MILDEW told anyone who would listen that *she* hosted Easter that year!

—Kara, *Washington, D.C.*

Dis-Carded

MILDEW is a card nut. She sends cards for Halloween, Valentine's Day, and St. Patrick's Day, and she sends multiple cards on birthdays. You name the holiday, she sends a card for it. But there's one holiday when she doesn't send a card . . . our wedding anniversary. I admit I find it very funny. After ten years of marriage I now fantasize about sending MILDEW a condolence card reading, "With Sympathy on the Loss of Your Son . . . to Marriage."

But it doesn't end there. MILDEW normally calls my husband every day, at least once a day—every day, that is, except one—our anniversary. Even *he* notices.

—Ava, *California*

Food Foibles

Food can bring a family together—you know, warm family get-togethers with lively conversation and the chance to catch up with each other. Or not.

Yummy

Whenever I invite MILDEW to come to our home for dinner, I work really hard to put together a great meal, pulling out all the stops. Like clockwork, as soon as I put the plate in front of her, but before she tastes anything, she says, "This is delicious." Then no more compliments the rest of the evening!

—Randy, *New Jersey*

Smokin'!

MILDEW often stays at our house for long weekends. One Friday, my husband put a meat loaf in the refrigerator before he left for work, and asked her to put it in the oven at 5 P.M. at 350 degrees. Because we both dislike greasy food, we use a double meat loaf pan to cook it. Holes in the bottom of the inside pan allow the fat to drip into the outside pan.

When I arrived home at 5:30, the house was filled with smelly blue smoke. MILDEW met me at the door and said, by way of greeting, "Your oven is so dirty that the grease is burning!" I opened the oven to discover the real cause. Because she didn't understand why anyone would need two pans, MILDEW had simply removed the bottom one and put the meat loaf in the oven. Grease was merrily dripping through the holes onto the bottom of the oven. It took me *hours* to clean up the mess. Oops!

—Jackie, *Illinois*

Cooking Light

MILDEW was visiting and decided to cook dinner that evening. Afterward, my husband casually mentioned that if he ate that much at every dinner he would start gaining weight. MILDEW turned to me saying, "Don't you make at least this much food every day?!" Meanwhile, she had made one entrée and I had made the rest of the meal!

—Sophie, *Canada*

Recycling

MILDEW is so thrifty that any soda my kids don't drink is poured right back into the two-liter bottle. *Ick!*

—Meredith, *Texas*

Sweet Tooth

Gravity has taken charge of MILDEW's figure, as it has for many of us. It hasn't with my mother, creating some mild ten-  sion. MILDEW was making the six-hour drive to visit us, and picked up some candy along the way. In her infinite wisdom, MILDEW decided to open the package with her teeth. The problem? She has dentures—and she broke one of her front teeth. Upon her arrival that afternoon we tried all the glues in the house, including Superglue, to fix the tooth. They would work for a while and then the tooth would fall out.

As luck would have it, I had invited my mother to join all of us for dinner that evening: a recipe for disaster at the best of times. When my mother knocked on the front door and started to walk in, MILDEW rushed to meet her. Unfortunately, the tooth fell out just as she reached the front door. MILDEW screamed and slammed the door in my mother's face, then rushed to the bathroom. It took quite a while to convince my mother that it was nothing personal. Likewise, it took some time to convince MILDEW that my mother would sit at the same table with her, even if she was missing a front tooth.

—Eleanor, *U.K. (United Kingdom)*

Tasty Treat

MILDEW told her entire family that at our first meeting (at a local restaurant) I ate a packet of Sweet 'N Low, packaging and all, for no reason. My husband has a great sense of humor and says, "If my mom says it happened, it *must* be true!"

—Allison, *Massachusetts*

Choco-LATE

One day MILDEW surprised me by giving me a box of Godiva chocolates. I was pregnant at the time, so they were a welcome treat. However, two weeks later, MILDEW called to ask if I had eaten the chocolates. "Yes, why?" I asked. It turns out that she had received the chocolates as a gift more than six months before. MILDEW was worried that the chocolates had gone bad and might have made me sick. I kept wondering why it took her two weeks to call me . . .

—Celeste, *Connecticut*

Steamed Spinach

After we announced our engagement I went on a serious diet to lose weight for the wedding. Soon after I began the diet, MILDEW invited us over for dinner. I asked my fiancé (now my husband) to remind MILDEW that I was dieting and wouldn't be eating meat or any fattening foods. When we arrived at MILDEW's the food was already laid out on the table—pot roast, mashed potatoes, noodle casserole, and bread with butter. I was stunned. My husband looked at his mom and asked what she had made for me. MILDEW ran into the kitchen and came out with a huge bowl of creamed spinach!

—Dara, *Massachusetts*

The Twenty-One-Year-Old Pie

This story takes place in 1999: "I know that apple pie is your favorite kind of pie, David, so I went out yesterday and bought one especially for you to eat today," MILDEW announces.

"Awesome! Thanks! Can I go get it?" asks David.

"Of course! It's in the downstairs fridge," replies MILDEW.

"Okay," says David. So he goes to retrieve the pie from the fridge.

"It looks kind of weird," David says.

"Maybe we should check the date on that; it looks like . . ." starts Mom.

"Ewwwww! It expired in 1978!" shouts David.

And so the pie goes into the trash. Now we check everything, and, really, a lot of food has expired. For example, the last time we went to visit MILDEW we checked the jelly and, lo and behold, it had an expiration date of "a while back."

—David (twelve years old) and his mom, *Illinois*

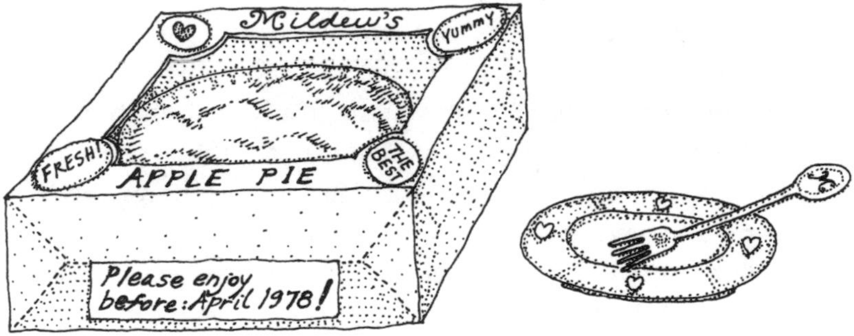
Mildew's
Yummy
Fresh!
The Best
APPLE PIE
Please enjoy
before: April 1978!

Hair of the Dog

Somehow MILDEW is under the impression that her sons love her turkey dinners. So every now and then I come home to a grocery bag hanging on my front door. Inside the bag is a whole cooked turkey wrapped in MILDEW's twenty-five-year-old gray dish towel.

The legs are always missing because my father-in-law loves turkey legs (he always takes them before anyone else can). Also in the bag is a container of MILDEW's famous gravy. Mmmm-mmm. The gravy has all the gross stuff from the neck and giblets. Yuck! She never removes anything from her gravy, so it's very lumpy and full of mysterious things. We've learned to never, ever open the container.

But let's put all this in some perspective here. The grossest part is *not* the fact that the turkey could have been on my door for hours, and it's *not* that the turkey is wrapped in her twenty-five-year-old dish towel. The grossest part has to do with her three big dogs, which run all over her kitchen. Everything in her house is full of dog hair—believe it or not, the turkey is covered in it. That's why we never even *look* at the turkeys anymore. We just take the bag off the door and put it in the garbage. She always asks how it was and

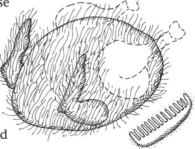

we always tell her it was great. We don't have the heart to tell her the truth. But the turkey really is *that* gross. When my husband was in college, MILDEW even used to mail him turkeys!

—Larissa, *North Carolina*

Jell-O Hell-o

I am a native New Yorker and I married a true southerner. The first time my husband Jack brought me home to meet his parents, MILDEW asked what I like to eat, to which I replied, "I like salad." When we sat down to dinner the first night, the meal consisted of chicken, potatoes, and a red Jell-O mold, which southerners call Jell-O salad. After dinner, my husband went into the kitchen to help his mother with the dishes. MILDEW immediately asked him why I had not touched the Jell-O salad. Jack replied matter-of-factly, "She likes green salad." Later that evening, the two of us laughed about the dinner and Jack assured me that there would be green salad the next evening. We sure were surprised when we sat down to dinner the next night—there sitting prominently in the center of the table was a ring of lime green Jell-O.

—Meryl, *Colorado*

Baby Blues

It's amazing how the birth of a child can speed the spread of MILDEW. While children can be one of life's greatest joys, the yin/yang of it is that keeping MILDEW at bay often becomes more difficult. The similarities in many of these stories are uncanny.

I'm in You, You're in Me

When I told MILDEW (who happens to think of *my* husband as *her* husband, too . . . another story in itself) that I was pregnant, she proudly announced, "I'm so excited! It's like *you're* pregnant, but *I'm* going to have your baby!" I cried.

—Eva, *Kansas*

I've Got a Secret

I must preface this story by saying that everyone in the family knows I have a *very* close relationship with my mother, and *not* with MILDEW. . . . When I became pregnant with my first child, my husband and I were adamant about keeping the pregnancy secret during the first trimester. Of course, both sets of parents were told about the pregnancy before we made the news public; and each was told to keep the news secret until we told them otherwise. Sometime during the first trimester, my parents were down in Florida and went out to dinner with my in-laws. Strangely, MILDEW had never called to congratulate my parents and had never made mention of the pregnancy, even when they got together for dinner. Toward the end of the evening, my mother finally decided to say something; so she asked, "So, what do you think of the pregnancy?" MILDEW replied, in a shocked tone, "You know???!!"

—Andrea, *Maryland*

E.P.T. Early Pregnancy Teller

I was exactly one-week pregnant when MILDEW happened by for a visit. Of course I had told my mother, but I was waiting until, oh, maybe the eighth month to tell MILDEW. While she was visiting she asked to use our upstairs bathroom, since the one downstairs was being redone. She came downstairs with this huge grin on her face and said (coyly), "Deborah," (she usually calls me Deb), "do you have something to tell me?" I panicked. How could she possibly know??? And then it dawned on me—she had looked in my bathroom trash can and seen the pregnancy test. Is nothing sacred?!

—Yvonne, *Oregon*

The Breast View

When I first tried breast-feeding I was very nervous. To make matters worse, MILDEW was standing next to me, watching intently. When the baby finally latched on, MILDEW reached over and pushed down on my breast so that she could see better. Eeeeww, gross! Can you imagine having your MILDEW touch your boob?

—Olivia, *Maryland*

Projection

I was at the hospital holding my new baby boy when MILDEW walked in. She looked at my son and said, "Now you'll understand the love a mother has for her son and how no one is ever going to be good enough for him." I was speechless.

—Alyssa, *Mexico*

What's the Frequency, Kenneth?

When I was pregnant with my son, MILDEW wanted us to name him after her husband, Ken. My husband and I, however, decided to name our son Jacob. MILDEW refused to accept this and proceeded to call our son Ken. What's up with that? She persisted in calling him by a name that wasn't even his! I've just recently had a second son, and now she calls *him* Ken instead (needless to say, that's not his name). What happens if we have a daughter?

—Gretchen, *Maine*

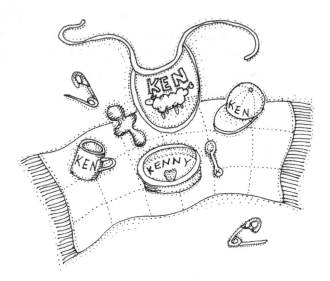

What About Me?

My son, who bears a strong resemblance to his father (to the joy of MILDEW), was born with clear blue eyes. When his eyes started to change color and obviously become the same color as mine, MILDEW announced, in front of a group of people, "How come his eyes look like yours? It's not like you had anything to do with him."

—Dina, *California*

Train Ride

Our son was six months old and waking up every two hours each night. For a change of scenery, we went to visit my mother—with disastrous results. A few weeks later it was Christmas and we just couldn't bear the thought of more traveling. So we decided to challenge convention and invite MILDEW to visit us for a change. No matter—she insisted that we visit her. She refused to come, saying the train ride would be too traumatic. Too traumatic? What about doing it with a baby?!

—Traci, *Australia*

Three-Card Monte

Soon after my child was born, MILDEW dropped off a gift of two baby outfits from her mother. They were in a box from a store I had never heard of. I later discovered that it was an exclusive children's boutique in the suburbs (we live in the city). I have to admit that I was surprised because MILDEW never gives us gifts from a department store, much less an exclusive boutique. And I knew that MILDEW bought the outfits on behalf of her mother, who was living in a nursing home at the time.

Anyway, as usual I did not like the outfits and wanted to exchange them. So I decided to be brave and take my child on his first car outing. Upon arriving at the suburban boutique, I struggled with the car seat/stroller contraption and worked up a good sweat. I finally made it into the store and breathlessly asked to exchange the outfits that were inside the box with the store's name on it. After an uncomfortable pause, the salesperson told me that the outfits were not from their store—the outfits were brands they didn't carry! Of course I was completely embarrassed, as well as infuriated.

I decided to tell MILDEW what happened in hopes of preventing it from happening again. Her response? "Oh, my mother's nurse must have bought the outfits one place and put them in a box from the other place." Yeah, like a nurse would go to all that trouble!

—Zoë, *Pennsylvania*

The Messenger

After our first child was born, MILDEW came to help for a few weeks. Unbeknownst to me, she was unhappy with my diet. When my husband and I took our daughter for her first checkup, out of no-where he asked the doctor if it was okay for me to eat chocolate while I was nursing. It turns out that MILDEW thought I was making a mis-  take as a new parent, and back then my husband didn't notice that he was being used as a messenger.

—Phoebe, *Virginia*

Unforgettable

MILDEW has described her birthing experiences for all three of her children so many times that I can recite them at will. I may forget my own experience when I have a child someday, but I am sure that I will never forget hers!

—Hannah, *Oregon*

. . . Plastics

My best friend on the East Coast decided to throw a surprise baby shower for me. She planned well in advance so that MILDEW (who lives on the West Coast) would be able to fly in. When my friend called to give her the date, MILDEW stated, "I have plastic surgery scheduled for that day. I'm getting a face lift for the baby!" I wonder what gift she plans to give my second child.

—Emma, *Maine*

Boat Ride

My son Andrew was just two years old when MILDEW and I took him to a little amusement park. At the park, there was a ride where the child sits in a little boat and goes around a tiny doughnut of water. MILDEW thought this was a great idea for Andrew. Me? I wasn't so keen on the idea. I didn't think he was old enough to go on by himself (the ride would not fit an adult). MILDEW kept quietly pressing her point, saying what a wonderful time Andrew would have on the ride, so I finally gave in and put Andrew in the boat. He was fine until it started to move. Then he became hysterical—and so did I—until the minute-long ride was over. I was certain he would suffer from separation anxiety for life. Years later MILDEW admitted that Andrew had been too young for the boat ride . . . Whoops!

—Anne Marie, *Michigan*

Framed

It was my baby shower and I was opening gifts . . . baby outfits, receiving blankets, stuffed animals. I opened the gift from MILDEW and it was a picture frame for my new baby. The frame came with a picture of a dog. I'm sorry, what's that? I didn't quite hear. The picture didn't

come with the frame? *You* put the picture in it? It's your dog? I don't get it. Is she equating my new baby with a dog? I'm so confused . . .

—Dana, *Connecticut*

I'm Sure She Meant It in a Nice Way . . .

Sometimes it's hard to understand the things that MILDEW says or does. You wonder: Is she trying to tell me something? Or does she just not know how it sounds? Hmmmm. It's tough to know.

I Like You, Too!

My husband recently started playing softball with a local league, and they play twice a week. A few days ago, MILDEW called to ask me if I was planning to go to my husband's game that night. When I said, "No, I don't think I can make it," she replied, "Oh, good. I guess I can go then!" Gee, thanks a lot.

—Sandra, *California*

Animal Crackers

I am a PETA member—no meat, no leather, no products tested on animals, right? When my husband told MILDEW that I am a vegan and PETA member, I guess she didn't understand what that meant. So when I met her for the first time she offered me a full-length rabbit coat. I'm sure she meant it in a nice way . . .

—Holly, *New York*

One-Liner

I was from the West Coast and getting married on the East Coast. MILDEW lives on the East Coast and I had no family to help me with wedding plans. That's when MILDEW decided to take a surprise trip out-of-town—so no planning help. But MILDEW *did* call me every day to report on her dress for the wedding and to discuss the hemline. I don't know how, but the wedding came off without a hitch, followed by a relaxing honeymoon at a tropical resort. While there, MILDEW called up to inform us that she had placed a wedding announcement in the *New York Times* and it was due to appear upon our return. Imagine my surprise when I read the announcement—*paragraphs* on her family and one little line about me.

—Gabriella, *New Jersey*

She's Wonderful

One time my husband and I and my in-laws went to a birthday celebration for a friend. The man being feted was someone I had dated in college. As we went through the receiving line, the man of honor greeted my MILDEW. He began extolling my virtues, at which point MILDEW interrupted and said, "If she's so wonderful, why didn't *you* marry her?" I was speechless.

—Noelle, *Utah*

Slim Fast

I think of this story every time I reach for fattening foods . . .
MILDEW was sitting at my kitchen table watching me race
around. I had worked all day, had a baby on my hip, a toddler
on the floor, and MILDEW had just "dropped by," expecting to
join us for dinner. As I moved from task to task—out-of-breath,
aggravated, and exhausted—MILDEW said, "Gee, with all the
running around you do, you'd think you would be skinny."

—Erin, *Minnesota*

Breath of Fresh Air

One day, out of nowhere, MILDEW gave me a bag filled with
seventeen different kinds of air fresheners. Was she trying to
tell me something?

—Veronica, *Illinois*

A Weighty Gift

When I was seven months pregnant we had Christmas at MILDEW's house. What did she get me? A scale. Yeah, a scale. When I opened it and in surprise said, "Oh my, a scale," MILDEW replied, "I thought you could use it." This came after a series of not-so-subtle hints that I had gained too much weight during my pregnancy (e.g., "Are you *sure* you aren't having twins?").

—Rebecca, *New Hampshire*

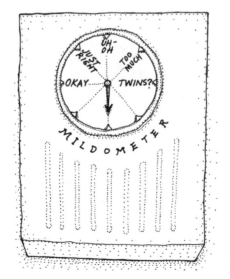

She's So Thigh

MILDEW gave me a Thigh Master for Christmas one year.

—Margot, *Connecticut*

Weight a Minute

I had been married for several months when MILDEW asked me when my husband and I thought we would try to get pregnant. When I told her that we were already trying, MILDEW said something about losing weight before getting pregnant because it would be harder to lose it after. Ummm, do I have a weight problem that I'm not aware of?

—Priscilla, *Texas*

By Accident

Years ago I was in a terrible car accident and totaled the car. I was in the hospital for five days with a broken nose and I was black and blue all over my face and body. One day MILDEW came to visit me in my semiprivate room. I was in the first bed, near the door. She walked right past me to the other patient's bed. After a moment MILDEW realized her mistake and came back to my bed, the first bed, at which point she said, "Hi. You look good!"

—Ilana, *Florida*

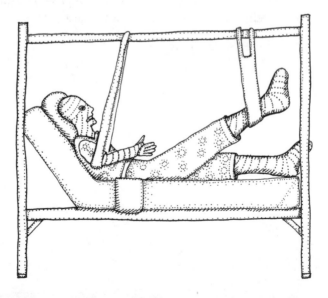

C.O.D.

Shortly after we were married, MILDEW went to Sweden on vacation. Before she left, MILDEW asked if there was anything she could bring back for us. We had received some lovely Kosta Boda glassware as wedding

gifts and wanted to complete our set. So I asked her if she could get us the missing pieces. She took down the information and seemed enthusiastic about the purchase. While she was still away a big package arrived from Sweden—C.O.D. I paid the mailman and haven't asked MILDEW for anything since.

—Robin, *Montana*

I'm Lonely?

What follows is a series of phone calls between a pregnant woman and her MILDEW. It's a shining example of how universal the MILDEW experience is.

MONDAY

MILDEW: So, what are you doing? How are you feeling?

Me: I'm fine. I was working on a freelance project.

MILDEW: Okay, just checking in.

TUESDAY

MILDEW: How are you?

Me : (puzzled) I am fine . . . same as yesterday.

MILDEW: When I was pregnant, I didn't have anyone around. I used to miss my folks.

Me : (politely laughing) Yes, that must have been hard.

MILDEW: You must be lonely. When are your parents coming?

Me : I'm not lonely since I have some work to keep me busy. My parents are coming tomorrow.

MILDEW: Oh, you are alone now?

Me : Yes . . . why?

MILDEW: Okay, bye-bye.

WEDNESDAY

MILDEW: Have your parents come yet?

Me : No, not yet. They will be coming this afternoon.

MILDEW: Oh! You are alone at home?

Me : Yes.

A few hours later . . .

MILDEW: Have your parents come?

Me : Yes. They've gone out for a bit.

MILDEW: You are alone?!!

Me : Yes. . . . But why are you calling me every day?

MILDEW: Why do you ask? I thought you were lonely!

Me : No, really, I'm not. But thank you anyway.

—Kali, *U.K. (United Kingdom)*

We Are Family

My husband of thirty-eight years was scheduled to have open heart surgery, so I told MILDEW that I wouldn't be able to visit her for the next week or so. Her reply? "Oh, I feel so bad for him. You know, he's almost like family!"

—Lori, *Missouri*

Bill and What's-Her-Name
June 1986

Fuzzy Wuzzy

You know those wedding photos where either the bride or the groom is fuzzy in the background, looking at their new spouse with that goofy look? Well, MILDEW decided to frame one of those shots from our wedding. Of course, I (the bride) am in the background and fuzzy, while my husband is in the foreground and very clearly in focus.

Normally, that wouldn't be so terrible. However, MILDEW made that photo the centerpiece of a large three-photo picture frame. On each side are other photos from the wedding . . . one of MILDEW's other son and his wife and one of MILDEW's daughter and her husband. The other spouses are clear and in the foreground of their pictures. So I am the only one of the six that is fuzzy and in the background.

When I pointed this out to my husband, he didn't like it either and talked to MILDEW about it. She still saw nothing wrong with it! I'm trying really hard not to read anything into it.

—Abby, *Wisconsin*

I Feel Pretty

Just after having my first child, MILDEW gave me a housecoat as a gift. You know, the zip-up-the-front, loose-fitting type of robe Aunt Edna would wear. I didn't know whether to laugh or cry. I'm guessing it was something she would pick out for herself, and, yes, the zipper would provide easy access for breast-feeding. But when you're only twenty-nine and already worried about losing 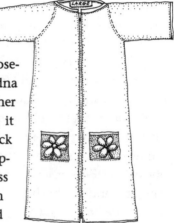 your sexuality, the last thing you want to do is dress thirty years older than you are. Thank goodness I was able to exchange it discreetly!

—Stacey, *Nebraska*

MILDEW Bloopers

Sometimes MILDEW acts in ways that are pretty darn surprising or just plain *uncomfortable*. When we witness these moments, well, that's what nervous giggles are for . . .

But I Swear. . .

One day, when my son was about eight years old, he asked me about swear words. I briefly told him which words were considered "bad." He immediately responded by telling me that those words couldn't be bad because "Grammy uses them all the time!"

—Mandy, *Pennsylvania*

Kind of Blue

At the age of sixty-eight MILDEW has just learned to use a computer. We've created a monster! She is addicted to e-mail and surfing the Internet, and now she keeps e-mailing me dirty jokes. I hate opening her e-mails because I get completely embarrassed. Why does she keep sending them to me?

—Lena, *India*

Cheater

MILDEW helps her favorite grandchild cheat when the child is playing games with my daughter! Last Christmas, the two girls were playing hide 'n' seek and MILDEW watched as my daughter hid. Then she told the favorite grandchild! She did this over and over again, and I just couldn't believe it.

—Amanda, *Massachusetts*

Citizen's Arrest

One day MILDEW took my two children, ages seven and ten, out for lunch. On the way, she was cut off by another driver. So she followed the car until it turned into a mall parking lot and parked. MILDEW pulled behind the car and got out. My children hid under the seat of the car as she proceeded to scream at the other driver and threaten to "citizen's arrest" him, as she apparently has the power to do in Colorado. My kids were mortified!

—Peggy, *Colorado*

Hide 'n' Seek

MILDEW always keeps me on my toes. Apparently, she didn't approve of my favorite old Pyrex measuring cup, so she bought me a new one. After MILDEW left my house to go home, I looked for the  old measuring cup, but she had brought it to her house to use as a backup!

—Nikki, *Wisconsin*

Missing Persons

When we moved into our apartment MILDEW came to visit. She went to use the bathroom and was gone for a *very* long time. After a while I went to see if she was okay. But she wasn't in the bathroom . . . Where did she go? I finally found MILDEW in my bedroom, going through my dresser drawers. I was shocked! Her response? "You're so neat on the outside, I wanted to see if you are as neat on the inside, too."

—Celia, *Georgia*

Hot Air Filter

MILDEW has this habit of "speaking out of turn." No issue is too small or too personal—she gives a play-by-play analysis of rocky marriages, wayward children, and personal health issues (not for the squeamish)—all behind the backs of the parties involved. After the analysis she is always sure to share her opinion. It's like having an advice columnist in the family (whether we want one or not!).

As you might guess, MILDEW has no filter. She talks about *very* personal issues—issues I'm sure no one wants her sharing with us. In fact, the surest way to spread news is to tell her that what you're saying is confidential. Like clockwork the whole family will know within a matter of days. What makes matters worse is that MILDEW remembers *every* detail of *every* problem back to the beginning of time. She recounts these stories again and again. And she doesn't stop. Ever. When she gets tired of our family secrets then she moves on to other families (whether we know them or not). I wonder what MILDEW says about us!

—Sofia, *Texas*

Belle of the Ball

MILDEW chose the dress she was going to wear to our wedding, and decided to model it for us three weeks before the big day (in 1998). She came down the stairs beaming, wearing a 1980's ice blue prom dress and hair high atop her head. "What do you think? Does it match your colors?" she asked.

Well, no, it didn't match our colors. It certainly didn't match what we imagined a mother-of-the-groom would wear. A forced smile was plastered on my face. I was horrified, as was my fiancé. Thankfully, I was also speechless.

"Is that all you found?" he asked.

MILDEW explained that this dress made her feel young. My fiancé was trying to maintain a straight face.

"You don't like it?" MILDEW was catching on. We were doomed.

"Well, I would like you to wear something a little more, um, classic," he muttered, while looking at his hands.

"Then *you* find me something!" She stomped off. We both sighed.

Two weeks later, with the wedding a few days away, MILDEW received a package with four dresses to choose from. She approved, we approved, and all's well that ends well.

—Shirley, *Maryland*

Whine and Cheese

Last year, MILDEW had a friend whose daughter was getting married in the town where I live. As it happens, the bride's father owns a small wine shop in town. MILDEW thought it would be clever to give the daughter a gift certificate for some wine from her father's store. I, of course, thought it was a cheesy idea. This girl probably has more wine than she could drink in a lifetime! But in an ongoing effort to get along, I decided to give MILDEW some agreeable-sounding response.

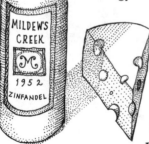

Apparently, that was the *completely* wrong strategy. She asked *me* to go the shop to buy the gift certificate! Since I was trying to be agreeable, I couldn't back out. Due to total embarrassment, though, I skulked into the store, trying to be inconspicuous. I strategically avoided the bride's father and got a salesgirl to help me. It was smooth sailing until she shouted (in her loudest salesgirl voice), "And who did you say the gift certificate was for?" I mumbled the daughter's name and then made sure to mention (at least 100 times) that I was doing this for my mother-in-law. I didn't want any credit for this idea.

—Carmen, *Michigan*

Good Taste

One day, MILDEW invited her sister to come see our new house and decided to play "hostess." Little did I know what that really meant. I went off to feed the baby, and when I was done I discovered MILDEW and her sister in my bedroom closet and all my dresser drawers open.

"What are you doing?" I inquired (not so nicely, I admit). "I just wanted to show my sister your good taste," MILDEW stammered. Now whenever MILDEW comes over I lock my bedroom door.

—Melissa, *Vermont*

False Teeth

MILDEW has false teeth. And I think that on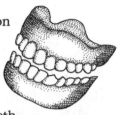
some level, she forgets that others don't.
Apparently, there are times when they
become uncomfortable. So we'll be walking down the street or sitting at a table,
and suddenly MILDEW will shift her teeth
until they almost come out. And she acts as if nothing is
askew. When she does this, I never know what to do. Do I
look away? Do I say something? Inevitably, I freeze—staring
at her with my mouth agape I'm sure. Why in the world does
she do that?

—Sherrie, *Massachusetts*

Mission Control

When a man gets married there is usually a passing of the baton, so to speak, from the mother to the wife. Sometimes that transfer goes smoothly and, well, sometimes it doesn't. Houston, we've got a problem . . .

A Brief Pause for Station Identification

Shortly before my wedding, MILDEW wanted to take me shopping. I was flattered, and went with her to Neiman Marcus. For our shopping trip I was wearing a pair of nice slacks and a Ralph Lauren shirt with the Polo insignia on it. While we were waiting for her personal shopper, MILDEW leaned in and whispered, "Now that you are marrying Robert, you need to dress appropriately for your new station in life." Then MILDEW had the personal shopper show me only silk blouses. Fuming, I agreed to buy a few; but of course from then on I'd only wear T-shirts when I knew I'd be seeing MILDEW.

—Isabel, *California*

Name Game

When I got married eight years ago I didn't take my husband's last name. MILDEW refuses to acknowledge this. She's in denial. We exchange e-mail and packages, and my full name is on them when they're sent. Yet MILDEW sends me e-mail and packages in return, always with my husband's last name, not mine. Will we ever get this straightened out?

—Jaime, *Ohio*

MILDEW JONES
5678 ANGELIC WAY
LEXINGTON KY 44123

JAIME ~~SMITH~~ Jones
1234 PATIENCE LANE
CINCINNATI OH 45215

No Good Deed Goes Unpunished

One winter we had a bad ice storm and there was a huge power outage in our area. My husband and I were lucky and got our power back in fourteen hours. However, MILDEW, who was living in the same general area, was not so lucky. To be kind, I invited MILDEW and my (grown) brother-in-law to keep warm by staying at our home for the night. Mistake! MILDEW allowed my brother-in-law to bring along two of his friends—without even asking first. And then MILDEW arrived with *six* loads of laundry to do. But it didn't end there. The next morning, MILDEW walked into our bedroom (where our washer and dryer are) without knocking—to warm my brother-in-law's clothes in our dryer! Whoever said fish and visitors smell after three days was being generous.

—Beth, *Maine*

P.S. I found out the next day that MILDEW not only had had wood for her fireplace so she could have kept warm at her own house, but she owns a generator so she could have had power throughout her house, too.

Only the Best

When my husband and I were looking for our first apartment, we had a very limited budget. Purely by coincidence (I swear), we were interested in a neighborhood not too far from MILDEW. But after looking, we realized that the rents were too high for us. Soon thereafter MILDEW called up and said, "I found you an apartment."

"Really?" I said. "Where? And how much is it?"

The apartment was a few blocks from hers and the rent was way beyond our budget—and I told her that we couldn't afford it.

MILDEW said, "Listen. My son is used to the very best."

It took all my self-control to keep from pointing out that he *has* the very best . . . (me).

—Molly, *New York*

In Absentia

Soon after we announced our engagement, MILDEW planned a big party for us. She arranged everything—caterer, flowers, music, and she sent out the invitations. The only problem was that she didn't tell us the date of the party until after the invitations went out. As luck would have it, I was in charge of a charity benefit that I had been working on for months. And I *had* to be there. MILDEW was flabbergasted. "What do you mean? Didn't you *tell* them your mother-in-law is throwing you an engagement party?!" And I'm thinking, "But of course—the world revolves around me."

Well, she didn't cancel the party (or change the date), so my fiancé went to our engagement party while I went to the charity benefit. What a way to start a relationship with MILDEW!

—Sylvie, *Maryland*

Alarmed

MILDEW normally wakes up at about 9 A.M. Jerry (my husband) normally wakes up at 5:30 A.M. to get ready for work. What does one thing have to do with the other? Well, after Jerry and I got back from our honeymoon MILDEW started set-ting her alarm clock early so that she could  call me at 5:30 every morning—to have no real conversation with me. It took me a while to catch on that MILDEW was calling to be sure I would wake up early to feed her son breakfast!

—Maya, *New York*

Who's Your Daddy?

One day I overheard MILDEW teaching one of her two-year-old grandchildren to call her "Mommy." She kept pointing to her own chest, saying "Mommy. Mommy." The child looked so confused; her eyes and mouth were wide open as she tried to make sense of it all.

—Tina, *Minnesota*

Bargain Baby

After being married for two years, my husband and I announced to his parents that I was pregnant with our first child (their first grandchild). Instead of congratulating us, MILDEW immediately exclaimed, "You can't be! I told the whole family you couldn't afford to have a baby yet. Now what will I tell them?!"

—Lydia, *Arizona*

Oh, Boy

Whenever my husband and I have family news, MILDEW complains that we never call her first. So when we finally got pregnant, guess who we called first? We were so excited to spring the good news on her. But before my husband could get it out of his mouth, she guessed. Deflated, my husband then shared the details, such as due date, appointments, etc. They chattered on the phone for fifteen minutes. Then MILDEW asked to speak to me.

"Hello?" I couldn't imagine why she wanted to talk to me after discussing all the details with her son.

"How are you feeling?" she asked.

I couldn't help but smile, thinking that we were finally going to be parents. "Fine, fine. A little anxious, but excited."

"That's good to hear." Long pause. "But you know, it *has* to be a boy. We need to carry on our family name." Okaaay. No pressure there.

—Lizette, *Michigan*

P.S. To MILDEW's great delight (and my relief), we had a beautiful baby boy.

Don't Ask, Don't Tell

When my husband lost his job and decided to stay home with the baby for a while, MILDEW's response was, "But what will I tell my friends?"

—Danielle, *Maryland*

By a Hair

One afternoon we were all on an outing and MILDEW was driving (my father-in-law was in the front passenger seat). My husband and I were in the backseat and I had my legs up on his lap.

I leaned in to whisper to him (at least I *thought* I was whispering), "Feel my legs. I actually shaved for the first time in a while."

Suddenly MILDEW piped in, "How am I ever gonna get more grandchildren?!"

—Natalie, *Massachusetts*

Hurry Up!

By the time we were engaged, my husband and I knew we wanted to have children. So we started trying a month or so before our wedding. Shortly after the wedding, MILDEW asked me when we were thinking of getting pregnant. I told her that we were very anxious to get pregnant and, in fact, had already started trying.

A few months later MILDEW learned that her friend's daughter was expecting—and her wedding had been the same day as ours. MILDEW asked us again when we would be making her a grandparent. We said we were doing the best we could, but that some things were not in our control. By this time I was starting to get a little touchy on the issue.

When the other happy couple had their baby, my husband and I had been married for almost two years (and we were seeking fertility advice). That's when MILDEW came to us with a very heartwarming story about how the father of the groom was quite ill and had told her what a great joy it was to see his grandchild. She pointed out that she did not want to have to be ill so that she, too, could enjoy the benefits of being a grandparent—and was wondering what she could do to persuade us to have children.

My husband tried explaining to MILDEW for the sixth time that we were, indeed, trying and that her questions were not helpful.

The moral of the story? So many to choose from . . .

- MILDEWs only hear what they want to hear.

- Don't tell anyone (especially MILDEW) when you start trying to conceive.

- Don't get married on the same day as MILDEW's friends' kids.

I am happy to report, though, that I now have two gorgeous girls!

—Jenna, *South Carolina*

Identity Crisis

MILDEW was pressuring my sister-in-law to have a baby and she just wasn't ready. So one day, MILDEW went through her drawers, found her birth control pills, and confronted her, screaming, "How dare you take these when I want a baby so badly!"

—Teri, *Oregon*

Redress

We had a family wedding coming up, so my preteen daughter and I went shopping for an outfit. She quickly found one that both of us loved. However, MILDEW was not at all pleased with it. She kept asking me, "Is that the look you had in mind for such a big day?" Then MILDEW added that she wasn't surprised by the outfit, as it clearly reflected my taste. I held my tongue.

After a few days, MILDEW couldn't help herself and said, "This is not the look I had in mind for my granddaughter," and took her shopping for a new dress. Not

surprisingly, my daughter disagreed with her choices, despite trying on an endless number of dresses. Predictably, my daughter went to the wedding happily wearing what she had originally chosen, even though it was not the look MILDEW had in mind.

—Alicia, *California*

Huh?

And then there are the stories that defy categorization. It's those indefinable moments from our indefatigable MILDEWs that really make us laugh. They may confound us, but isn't that half the fun? Okay, maybe fun isn't the right word . . .

Double Standard

One winter, I had a very bad case of the flu and so did my sister-in-law Libby. When my mother came to visit me, she ordered me to "stay in bed and don't move for several days." After visiting my sister-in-law, my mother said to me, "That Libby is a lazy good-for-nothing. She never gets out of bed, the kitchen is a mess, and the kids are hungry!"

—Noa, *New York*

Sympathetic

Whenever someone is sick, MILDEW says she has the same illness—even cancers and rare diseases. It's funny, though . . . she has never been in a hospital.

—Simone, *Connecticut*

The Poop Scoop

I don't know if it's just my MILDEW, but every conversation she has seems to incorporate her bathroom habits. We all know when, where, and how often MILDEW goes to the bathroom. She either goes too much or too little, and there are endless descriptions that we all must endure. Much to their embarrassment, she also likes to discuss the bathroom habits of her children when they were young (my husband is always amazed at how often these stories are repeated). Does anyone else think this is odd?

—Maggie, *Texas*

Bad News Bear(er)

For some reason, MILDEW loves spreading bad news. I don't know what it is, but if it's bad or sad, she loves to share it with *everyone*. A typical conversation:

MILDEW: I am *so* upset.

Me: Why?

MILDEW: Do you remember Mrs. D'Amico?

Me : No.

MILDEW: Yes you do. She was at your wedding.

Me : No, I don't remember her.

MILDEW: Yes you do. She was wearing the purple dress with sequins.

Me : Well, maybe (I say to keep the story moving).

MILDEW: I knew you'd remember her. Well, her second cousin's son was (in a whisper—even though we're completely alone) arrested.

Me : For what?

MILDEW: That's not important, but she's devastated.

Me : You don't know what he was arrested for?

MILDEW: Did you get the fruit cake I sent?

Me : Yes, but . . . I, uh . . . okay.

—Shannon, *Massachusetts*

Now You See Her, Now You Don't

When I first met my husband, MILDEW had a cleaning woman working for her five days a week. When MILDEW's daughter Susie got married, MILDEW paid for the cleaning woman to go to Susie's house one day a week. When Susie had a baby she got her two days a week. When my husband and I got married, nothing. When we had a baby, MILDEW paid for the cleaning lady to come to my house one day a week. But Susie got upset with that arrangement, so MILDEW paid the cleaning lady *not* to go to my house to clean. What's that about?

—Patsy, *Washington*

Identity Theft

Oh, I remember a funny story. At my wedding, my husband and I didn't want to pose for family photos—we wanted the natural look of the wedding. Apparently MILDEW was frustrated with this. So she found my veil and flowers, which I had abandoned when I got up to dance, and put them on to pose for the photographer. Actually, maybe that's not so funny . . .

—Jade, *Maryland*

To Dye For

MILDEW dyes her hair gray. Yup, you read it right—she dyes it gray. She's only fifty-two and her hair is still brown, but for some reason this is what she does. Nope, we don't know why. It's a family mystery.

—Marissa, *New Jersey*

Car Appreciation

My husband recently went to Florida to visit his folks, and was told that the adventure for the day would be a family get-together since everyone wanted to see him. First, they picked up his aunt, who said to MILDEW, "You're so lucky your son comes to visit." MILDEW said, "Well, if you paid for your son to come, you'd get visits, too." (Note: my husband paid his own way.) The aunt said, "Well, if I had your money, I'd pay." And so it went. By the time they arrived at their brother's home, the sisters weren't speaking.

At their brother's condo, my father-in-law started to pull into an emergency parking space. His brother-in-law told him not to park there. After arguing with him, the car was reluctantly moved—but then they weren't speaking either.

They went upstairs for dinner. The uncle's second wife then proceeded to "innocently" needle everyone. Since it was her home and her food, the family couldn't tell her off; however, they stopped speaking to her. So now you have six adults who aren't speaking to each other, and my husband, who is desperately trying to keep the conversational ball, if not rolling, at least in play.

After the very quiet ride home, they arrived at my in-laws' apartment. MILDEW said to my husband, in all seriousness, "Don't you wish you lived here and could spend more time with family?"

—Janice, *Iowa*

P.S.: My husband came home and said, "I am so lucky I'm married to you. What can I do for you to show my love and gratitude?" I said, "I want a Mazda Miata like Pam's." (Pam is our daughter.) He said, "Done." Whenever I drive it, I thank MILDEW for being who she is—it has served me well.

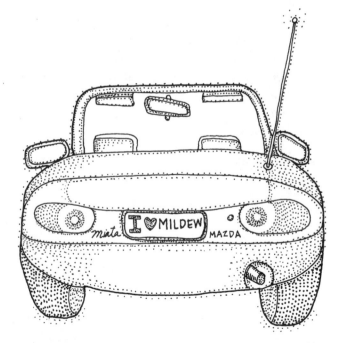

The Detective

I like to do crafts and have been known to ask stores for discontinued wallpaper books to use. One morning, MILDEW came over for brunch and saw a children's wallpaper book in my living room. She took one look at it and her jaw dropped—she was convinced I was pregnant. MILDEW stood there with her mouth agape and started smiling. I calmly assured her that the wallpaper was for my art projects, adding, "Believe me, if it were true, you certainly wouldn't find out like this." Somehow, she couldn't let go of the fantasy and began writing her own script. She decided that I had had a miscarriage, and she saw it as her job to console me. I couldn't stop giggling and just kept repeating over and over that I was not, nor had I ever been, pregnant.

—Betty, *Vermont*

Gender Bender

MILDEW buys my daughter boy's clothing. The clothes have soccer balls and footballs on them. I don't understand it. It must be pretty hard to find the only pair of "Powerpuff Girls" pajamas that look like they're for boys, with sports equipment and even race cars on them. To clarify, my daughter loves to wear makeup and she takes ballet lessons. She isn't even into sports.

—Kelly, *Pennsylvania*

How Practical!

While making some final wedding arrangements, MILDEW started telling me about the dress she would be wearing. She told me she'd had the dress for almost twenty years and couldn't wait to wear it again. Then for some unknown reason MILDEW told me that she wouldn't be having her gown cleaned before the wedding because "it's just going to get dirty that night. I'll have it cleaned after."

—Amy, *Utah*

Dialing for Dinner

My brother-in-law just got engaged and MILDEW is already going full throttle with wedding plans. She called me and "suggested" that my husband and I host a family dinner two nights before the wedding.

"It will be just family," she assured me.

"Just family?" I was incredulous. I have a full-time job and two small children. So there are four of us, five first cousins, aunts, uncles, my sister-in-law, MILDEW . . . you get the picture. By the time I finished counting, I was up to thirty people.

"Don't worry. I'll help," MILDEW responded.

Well, um, yeah, but I couldn't help remembering all the dinners where she didn't. Her idea of home entertaining is ordering in. Even my husband asked, "How does she plan on helping? By dialing the phone?"

—Alexandra, *Wisconsin*

Thrifty

A few weeks before my very formal wedding, MILDEW was in the hospital briefly. At one of our visits, she handed me a stack of the little plastic measuring cups used to dispense her pills each day. MILDEW suggested that I use them for serving wine to the wedding guests.

—Sydney, *Minnesota*

Toxic Shock

MILDEW loves to shop at flea markets. When we first had kids, she'd buy them lots of gifts there. That meant that every time she'd bring a gift, I'd have to go through my vetting process:

- Does it say what ages it's appropriate for?
- Is it nontoxic?
- Is it washable?

With my three-year-old waiting in the wings, I'd typically find a large, clear label with the following warnings:

- For ages 6+
- Toxic and permanent staining possible

Even better were the times when the label was in a foreign language. Inevitably, I'd have to be the bad guy and nix the toy. That was usually MILDEW's cue to insist that she hadn't seen the label. For the rest of the visit MILDEW would be annoyed with me because her gifts were not returnable. I can understand if this happened once. But I swear, it happened at every visit for at least two years until, at last, the gifts started coming from KB Toys.

—Giselle, *California*

Sunny Days

It was early summer and MILDEW had just returned from her winter in Florida. I was trying to put together our annual "welcome home" celebration and asked MILDEW to choose which day would be more convenient for her: Saturday or Sunday. She wouldn't commit, so I was getting frustrated. After a few days, I told her that we needed a decision so that we could plan the rest of the weekend for the kids. No response. Finally, my husband called MILDEW and she said, "I'll come whichever day is sunny." Huh? When we asked for clarification she responded, "I took tennis lessons in Florida and I want to show the kids what I learned." Please note: My kids are all under the age of eight. Somehow, I don't think they'll appreciate the finer points of a forehand . . .

—Abra, *New Jersey*

Assault & Battery

MILDEW walked in and the first thing she said was, "I bought a present for the kids, but I know you're not going to like it." Well, *that* didn't sound good. And I thought to myself, "Why did you buy it if you knew I wouldn't approve?" But discretion is the better part of valor, so I bit my tongue. After a sigh I resigned myself to the inevitable and asked, "What is it?" She immediately produced a small toy car wash with millions of pieces. Even better, she demonstrated that the car wash fills up with soap and water, making a huge mess.

Now keep in mind, I have two sons: a five-year-old and a thirteen-month-old who puts *everything* into his mouth. I bit my tongue again as my five-year-old began squealing in excitement about his new toy. That was right about the time I read the box and saw that it needed a nine-volt battery. To MILDEW I said, "Did you bring a battery?"

"Don't *you* have any?" she demanded. Predictably, I had no batteries, my son cried, and somehow MILDEW was mad at *me*."

—Leah, *Pennsylvania*

Equal Opportunity MILDEW

Although the primary focus of our book has been on women and their bouts of MILDEW, we do realize that men have MILDEW, too. It's just more challenging to get them to talk about it. It seems that men don't commiserate with one another the way women do. You have to dig a little deeper with them. Acknowledging that you have a problem is the first step to conquering it, and frankly, many men are in denial. For us, the key to tapping into the male MILDEW experience is being in mixed company. Whenever we start discussing MILDEW, we're amazed at how easily and naturally men jump right in with their own stories. It just goes to show that no one is immune. Be afraid. Be very afraid. Now, tales from the other side . . .

X-Ray Vision

My wife and I went on a weekend getaway, and we had MIL-DEW take care of our dogs. Inspiration and x-ray vision apparently kicked in while we were away, because that's when she decided that there must be nice hardwood floors underneath our carpeting. We returned to our rental apartment with the floors stripped bare of carpet, revealing wood planks and tack boards. It took us weeks to install a new floor!

—Tony, *New York*

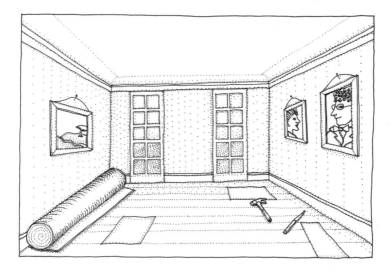

Right Out From Under Us

When my wife and I moved into a smaller place for a few years, we stored some of our things at MILDEW's. Among those things were several beautiful rugs. About a year later she had a flood. Her insurance company was great and took care of all the necessary cleaning and repairs. Until our first post-flood visit, though, we had no idea that the repairs included replacing her carpeting with hardwood floors. We also didn't know that she felt entitled to our rugs and redecorated her home using them. Even when we moved into a larger home, we never got them back. She still has my rugs!

—Brian, *Connecticut*

Forgiven

It was the first time I was going to visit my wife's parents at their home. The day was bursting with possibilities. I am Jewish, which her parents knew. They both happen to be Catholic and German. Better yet, my father-in-law is a veteran WWII German soldier. But wait, it gets better—my mom is a Jewish refugee who came to this country in 1951. In other words, the stage was set for a wonderful visit—and WWIII.

On the first day, out of nowhere, MILDEW approached and presented me with a hardcover coffee table book. It was about a French cardinal who converted from Judaism to Catholicism. MILDEW explained how the book shows that the Catholic Church is accepting of all people. I took this as a not-so-subtle message to convert. She then went on to assure me that the Catholic Church has forgiven the Jews for the crucifixion of Christ. I felt like a deer caught in the headlights. Nothing else was said for the remainder of our stay.

—Ross, *Illinois*

To "What's-His-Name":
Merry Christmas.
~The Smiths

Sock It to Me

MILDEW didn't want her daughter to marry me—the whole town, much less the family, had made that perfectly clear. But once we were married, I thought she would soften a bit. Apparently, I had miscalculated. For our first Christmas, MILDEW, who was from California, sent her gifts to us in New Jersey. At the time, MILDEW was working in a fabulous clothing store. Box upon box arrived, and on Christmas morning we opened them. One after the other had my wife's name on it, and each held a beautiful article of clothing. Finally, there was a box with my name on it. Only one box, mind you. What did I receive? One pair of green socks.

—Jeremy, *New Jersey*

Wet (Pig-in-a) Blanket

My fiancée, with the help of MILDEW-to-be, took care of all our wedding plans—I admit that it was a blessing. They made all the decisions and I was happy to stay out of it. But I had one request. Only one. I *really* wanted to have pigs-in-a-blanket and baby lamb chops for appetizers. That was it. That's all I wanted. My fiancée agreed, so I thought it was all settled. Boy, was I wrong. When we met with the caterer we were asked if there was anything specific we wanted to serve at the dinner. So I told them. MILDEW shot me a fierce look and announced that pigs-in-a-blanket were passé and baby lamb chops wouldn't work because there would be no place for the guests to put the bones. So, no pigs-in-a-blanket and no baby lamp chops . . . But at my wife's surprise thirtieth birthday party guess what we served?

—Josh, *Pennsylvania*

Marital Accounting

Early in my marriage I quickly recognized a pattern of over-spending by my wife whenever she shopped with her mother—who also happened to employ her. MILDEW had done very well for herself professionally, and had become the major breadwinner in her household. As a result, she denied herself nothing and was a good-natured advocate of the marital accounting philosophy of "What's mine is mine and what's yours is ours." I tried hard to convince my wife to limit her spending sprees while we were trying to save for a home. But MILDEW devised a tidy counterstrategy: Whenever an over-the-top purchase appeared at the house, my wife dutifully stated, "My mother paid for it," or "My mother split it with me." It took a while before I realized that some of my wife's paychecks were suddenly smaller, and that MIL-DEW was simply using her own version of GAMILAP, or Generally Accepted Mother-In-Law Accounting Practices. Where was Sherron Watkins when I needed her?

—Rob, *New York*

Clean Sweep

MILDEW prided herself on her housekeeping—both cleanliness and tidiness were paramount to godliness. The barbs we received on our housekeeping (or lack thereof) were polite, but never-ending. Imagine my excitement, then, when my toddler mumbled something about the furry pull toy under Grammy's rocking chair, and we all discovered that the rodent being pulled by its tail was neither stuffed nor even recently deceased. This little field mouse had a serious case of rigor mortis, and put a permanent stop to any critiques about *our* housekeeping.

—Greg, *Massachusetts*

Pyramid Scheme

Ten years ago my in-laws were in a very bad car accident. MILDEW was okay, but my father-in-law (coincidentally, an orthopedic surgeon) had to stay off his leg for six months while it healed. After the six months, MILDEW had the great idea that we should all go on a celebratory recuperation trip together. My father-in-law hadn't walked unaided for months, yet MILDEW's idea for the perfect trip was to go visit Egypt. Mind you, they were shooting tourists at the time—but that meant there was plenty of availability and good rates! So for my father-in-law's recuperation trip we hiked to the Great Pyramids and climbed through underground tunnels to the tombs of the pharaohs. By the time we returned home I think my father-in-law needed another six months to recover from the "recuperation trip!"

—Elliott, *Michigan*

The Invisible Man

Soon after we married I went to meet my mother-in-law for the very first time. I admit that I was very nervous. What I didn't realize was how upset MILDEW was that her daughter had married me. The whole time I was there MILDEW never acknowledged me—she kept referring to me as "him!" This went on for years (until we had children, actually).

—Michael, *Illinois*

Heads I Win, Tails You Lose

Every year for my wife's birthday MILDEW gives her an elaborate (and expensive) birthday present. But when *my* birthday comes around, MILDEW always gives me a gift that my wife has requested for the house. For example, last year my wife got a really nice, expensive coat, while I got a fancy crystal bowl that my wife had wanted. I've always wondered why MILDEW doesn't just buy my wife what she wants outright, instead of giving it to me as a "gift." Or better yet, why doesn't MILDEW give me a gift that I might want? I've decided that next year I'll plan ahead and have my wife tell MILDEW that she really wants a flat-panel television!

—Andy, *Virginia*

———*ww*———

Strategies:
Wipe That MILDEW Away!

*Be kind to your mother-in-law
and if necessary pay for her
board at some good hotel.*
—Josh Billings

*Happy is she who marries
the son of a dead mother.*
—James Kelly, Complete Collection
of Scottish Proverbs, 1721

*I haven't spoken to my mother-
in-law for eighteen months.
I don't like to interrupt her.*
—Attributed to Ken Dodd

The Real Thing

We did a lot of digging to provide our fellow MILDEW sufferers with the best available strategies for inhibiting the spread of MILDEW. We were able to compile and combine the latest research into the suggestions below. It is important to note that this information comes directly from industry and governmental sources. The wording remains virtually unchanged.

When building a new home, MILDEW issues should be addressed from the outset in order to avoid future problems. Regular airing [with your husband] can prevent or slow MILDEW's growth. MILDEW is an intrusive fungus. And although there are MILDEW inhibitors that can help to control MILDEW, there can be MILDEW resistance.

How to keep MILDEW at bay? Sometimes the solution can be quite involved. There is no widespread, available and usable information on this issue so far. But the demand for optimal living standards is growing. In the meantime, the best way to handle the toxic conditions is to dilute toxicity levels by using a MILDEW remover, of which there are several options. A MILDEWcide is a chemical that retards the growth of the MILDEW fungus.

Chemical MILDEW *removers can be effective, but are highly toxic—be sure to wear rubber gloves and have proper ventilation. An alternative is to use vinegar—a very effective* MILDEW *remover. Just fill a spray bottle with some vinegar and spray!*

Over the years, MILDEW veterans have devised numerous strategies to prevent or at least contain MILDEW outbreaks. As a public service, we share some of them in this chapter.

DISCLAIMER: These strategies are accompanied by *no* guarantees of effectiveness. Please use discretion in reading the following subject matter. Some content may not be suitable for all readers, and may appear extreme and overly dramatic in nature.

Sometimes You Feel Like a Nut

She's Da Bomb

Woe is Wafa Mustafa, a [Chicago] woman who faces sentencing next month for making a phony bomb threat that diverted a Chicago-bound Royal Jordanian jet. Mustafa told a federal court judge that she was desperate to prevent a visit by her . . . mother-in-law, who was one of the 183 passengers on the plane. The mother-in-law made it eventually, but Mustafa's problems are far from over. The twenty-six-year-old woman is looking at two to eight months in the slammer, a penalty that probably beats Thanksgiving dinner with that family. Sure, it's an extreme tale.

—Jean Davidson, "On the Outs with the Ins?"
Chicago Tribune, November 17, 1996

Gap Appeal

MILDEW happens to have terrible taste in gifts. It's become quite a source of humor in my family. After years of receiving these one-of-a-kind, non-returnable items, we finally had a chance to effect a "taste adjustment." My sister had just had her second child and MILDEW mentioned that she wanted to send a gift—what should she send her? Since my sister lives in a different city, I strongly urged MILDEW to buy something at the Gap, and I went into a long monologue on the merits of buying gifts at the Gap. Thankfully, she took my advice. More important, in an act of sibling solidarity, my sister wrote a thank-you note that included a long, exaggerated discussion on how wonderful Gap clothes are and how everyone nowadays buys their children's clothes there. All this in the hopes of preventing future nonreturnable, indescribable gifts.

—Brianna, *Florida*

See No Evil

The best remedy for MILDEW I have found is avoidance.

—Anonymous

Out of the Closet

This isn't one of my proudest moments, but it worked. Back when I was living in an apartment building, my mother had come to visit. We had been out shopping and were coming in the back door of my building when we suddenly heard MILDEW's voice. Panic! Ever the mature women, my mother and I ran into the package room and hid in a closet until we heard her leave. I think the doorman thought we were a little odd, but a big tip at Christmas kept him quiet.

—Shawna, *New York*

Sometimes You Don't

Below are a few bits of practical advice and recommenda-
tions that have been used by MILDEW sufferers with varying
degrees of success. While some strategies help avoid MILDEW
outbreaks, others help alleviate the situations with humor.
Warning: the humor may be one-sided.

1. Never answer the telephone during
   her regular calling times.
   Answering machines are
   particularly useful for
   MILDEW prevention.

2. Even better, get
   Caller ID!

3. If you get caught
   answering her call, we recommend
   the following methods for getting off the phone:

   • Ring your own doorbell.

   • Pretend you have company and talk to the
     nonexistent guest.

   • Run the shower, turn on the hair dryer, and say,
     "I just got out of the shower!"

- Get your dog to bark and tell her that Rover needs to go out for a walk.

- Tell her you hear the baby just waking up from his/her nap.

- Pretend you *are* your answering machine.

4. If you just can't get off the phone, ask lots of open-ended questions so that MILDEW does all the talking (and be sure to have a good magazine handy to entertain yourself).

5. If you need to call MILDEW and you have either call waiting or two lines, call a friend first and have her call you when you are on the phone with MILDEW. The following are potentially good excuses for taking the other call:

- It's your friend, who is in tears.

- It's your husband.

- It's the office.

- The gas company called and there's a gas leak.

- It's long distance from Australia.

- It's the President.

6. Or call MILDEW from the car and soon after tell her you've got to go because traffic is getting bad.

7. Have your husband call MILDEW from work or from his car (this is known as a preemptive strike).

Dead Zone

My husband drives to work every day. Because he uses his cell phone so much, he has discovered a dead zone where his calls are always disconnected. Soon after discovering it, he decided to use it to limit the length of his phone conversations with his mother. So now, five minutes before entering the dead zone, he'll call her (preemptive strike). And like clockwork, the call ends. It's funny, but don't you think after two years of this MILDEW would catch on?

—Kayla, *New Jersey*

8. Try not to let MILDEW know your schedule.

9. If you *must* let MILDEW know your schedule, give her the times when the kids will be home with the baby-sitter.

10. Never, ever give MILDEW your office or cell phone numbers.

11. . . . or the keys to your house!

12. If you live in an apartment building that has a doorman, tip him *very* well so that if MILDEW stops by unannounced, the doorman will say you aren't home.

13. Whenever possible, do not sit next to MILDEW at social gatherings.

14. If MILDEW is embarrassing you in a public place, stand behind her and roll your eyes (don't let your husband know you do this). Okay, we admit that this strategy is immature; but it sure does make us feel better!

Dazed and Confused

We've been asked many times, "Once you have MILDEW, is there any way to get rid of it?" Well, that's the toughest question there is. Maybe you can anonymously send her a copy of this book. Perhaps if she takes the quiz and reads a few stories she will have an epiphany—she may become enlightened and change her behavior forever! Then again, maybe not . . .

There are a number of MILDEW situations for which we have no easy answers. Sometimes we're just as bewildered as the next person. What follows are a few of those challenging situations and our confused, possibly immature attempts to survive them with some shred of grace and/or dignity.

Happy Mother's Day?

How do you buy MILDEW a Mother's Day card? I mean, what, exactly, do you want it to say? It's so . . . Well, it's just so . . . shhhhh, don't tell anyone we said this, but . . . it's so hypocritical, isn't it? Happy Mother's Day? to MILDEW? Okay, so here's how we've handled this holiday of conflicting emotions.

1. Just play it safe by choosing a card that says simply "Happy Mother's Day." They can be hard to find, but they're usually on the bottom near the "You're Just Like a Mother to Me" cards—don't mix them up!

2. If you have children, have them make the card. You can start doing this as early as age one. Just give them paper, a marker, and let them scribble away.

3. Tell your husband that he needs to buy the card since it's *his* mother.

Holy Day

My MILDEW is very into Mother's Day. For her, it is the holiest day of the year—even more important than Christmas and Easter. She's really into the cards that have all those poems and sentimental sayings. My first Mother's Day as a wife, I spent forever staring at the card rack—all those cards that didn't describe my mother-in-law. I finally found one with a bouquet of flowers on it that said, "Happy Mother's Day." When she opened it she glared at me, but then she gave me an air kiss. I think I have given her the exact same card, or at least a variation of it, every year since.

—Sabrina, *California*

What's-Her-Name (or You Can Call Me Ray)

What do you call *your* MILDEW? Sometimes we look with envy at those women who can call their mothers-in-law "Mom." But MILDEW is a certain type of mother-in-law. And again we ask, "What do you call her?" Not Mom. Huh-uh, not a chance. If her last name is Smith, do you call her Mother Smith? Nope; sounds strangely Victorian. You can try the dubious strategy of using her first name, but sometimes that doesn't seem right either.

Our answer: Don't call her anything at all. You can accomplish this by one or any combination of the methods listed below.

- Strategically position yourself so that you are always within range of making eye contact.

- Just wait until she looks at you (not always practical if you need to get her attention right away).

- Wait until she starts a conversation with you.

- Tap her on the shoulder.

If none of these work:

- Wait until you have children—then you can use whatever name they have for her.

- Mumble her first name.

No Name

For ten years, I avoided calling MILDEW anything. I certainly wasn't calling her "Mom." You can really get away with it for quite some time. One day, soon after I had a baby, she came to help. The baby spit up and she was in the den. I couldn't yell "Hey, you, can I have a diaper?" into the next room. So I started calling her by her first name. It still makes me uncomfortable, though.

—Paige, *Missouri*

Good Behavior

The last time MILDEW came to visit, I told her that my friend was collecting stories about mothers-in-law who don't listen and who annoy their daughters-in-law. After that she behaved noticeably better than she ever has. I don't know how long it will last, but I'm certainly going to remind her of your book each time she visits!

—Jan, *California*

CHAPTER SIX

MILDEW Musings

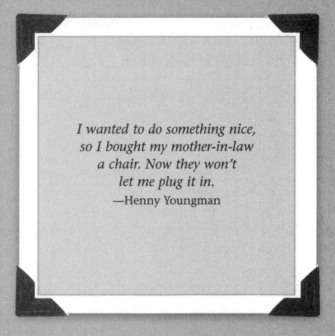

*I wanted to do something nice,
so I bought my mother-in-law
a chair. Now they won't
let me plug it in.*
—Henny Youngman

*A*s creators of the MILDEW concept, it's ironic that we have each been blessed with sons of our own. Both of us have a deep-seated fear that we will ultimately turn into MILDEWs. In the dark of the night, when our thoughts are our own, the fear seeps in. Little by little, the self-doubt and worry stake their claim. How do we avoid becoming MILDEWs? Well, we're hoping that awareness and having a good memory will help. Following are some helpful hints, food for thought, and because we can't help ourselves, more things to giggle over.

Italy Is My Favorite Country!

Italy court rules hellish in-law justifies divorce.

ROME, Fri March 14, 2003 (Reuters)–The mother-in-law from hell is the butt of jokes and comedies the world over.

In Italy, she is officially a cause for divorce.

The country's highest appeals court on Thursday upheld a ruling that granted a woman from Vasto in southern Italy divorce on the grounds of "excessive and inappropriate interference of the husband's parents in the private life of the couple."

"My husband was his mother's slave. He would hang on her every word while she criticized everything about me—my makeup, my diet, the way I was bringing up my daughter," the woman told the court.

The woman was awarded custody of her daughter and a generous alimony to compensate her for not being allowed to work after she was married.

The ex-husband has returned to live with his mother.

—Reprinted with permission from
Reuters, copyright © 2003

"Mother-in-Law" Fish

There is a fish called the Mother-in-Law Fish. It has a huge mouth and is hideous . . . I caught one in Alaska once. There is a real name for the fish, but I don't know what it is. You could probably find it on the Web.

—Kate, *Washington*

Thanks, Kate. Don't mind if we do! This is what we found through our Google search:

According to Captain Mike's Charters in Homer, Alaska, Irish Lords are often called the "mother-in-law fish" because of their very large mouths. "You never know what that tug on the line is going to bring," says Captain Mike.

—www.captmike.com/halibut.htm

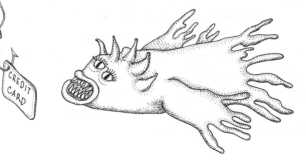

The Mother-in-Law Fish moniker refers to many different fish species the world over, from Florida to Alaska to Australia. Whatever the exact species—Irish Lords, Blubber Lips, Oyster Toadfish—the label of Mother-in-Law Fish invariably refers to a fish with bulging eyes, a big mouth, and spine-tipped fins. Uncanny!

And no humor book on mothers-in-law would be complete without a few jokes. Here are a few we think are especially amusing.

Long Life

A middle-aged man was visibly shaken when his doctor told him that he had only six months to live. "What will you do for your last six months?" asked the doctor.

The man thought for a few minutes and then replied, "I think I'll go live with my mother-in-law."

Surprised, the doctor asked, "Of all people in the world, why would you want to live with your mother-in-law?"

"Because it'll be the longest six months of my life!"

Charity Begins at Home

The president of a service club asked his new member, "Would you like to donate something to the home for the aged?" The new member replied, "Yes, my mother-in-law."

Driving You Crazy

They say the definition of ambivalence is watching your mother-in-law drive over a cliff in your brand new luxury car.

Airport Security

I was at the airport flying from home to meet my husband. When I checked in at the ticket counter, the agent asked me the usual security question, "Do you have any packages that you didn't pack yourself?" I told her that my mother-in-law had given me a package to take to her son (my husband). She looked at me very closely and asked, "Does she like you?"

Television Shows

*The Mothers-in-Law**

The Mothers-in-Law television series aired on NBC for two brief seasons from 1967 to 1969. The show was primarily about the relationship between two sets of in-laws, and in particular the two mothers-in-law, Eve and Kaye. The show's premise: Eve and Herb Hubbard are the next-door neighbors of Kaye and Roger Buell. The Hubbards' daughter, Suzie, marries the Buells' son, Jerry.

There were many *I Love Lucy*–esque themes—no coincidence since the executive producer was Desi Arnaz. However, a few episodes would make any MILDEW-sufferer giggle and nod knowingly.

Episode #2: "Everybody Goes on a Honeymoon"
The kids (Jerry and Suzie) are on their honeymoon—which ends quickly when they run into their mothers-in-law. *Early MILDEW indicator—there's a fungus among us.*

Episode #5: "The Newlyweds Move In"
When Jerry and Suzie move into the apartment over the Hubbards' garage, the mothers-in-law promise not to interfere in their kids' lives. *Surprise! They're caught snooping when they get stuck in the automatic garage door.*

Episode #17: "The Kids Move Out"
When Eve and Kaye meddle once too often, Jerry and Suzie decide to move out of the garage apartment. *We saw that one coming!*

The Mothers-in-Law television series is copyrighted by Desilu, too, LLC. The above-mentioned episodes were written by Madelyn Davis and Bob Carroll, Jr.

How's Your Mother-in-Law?

Also in 1967 (it was a good year for mothers-in-law), there was a mother-in-law television game show called *How's Your Mother-in-Law?* Wish we had played before we got married!

Rules: Three mothers-in-law competed for a $100 cash prize. Each had a celebrity "defense attorney." Ten singles served as a jury, deciding which woman they'd rather have as a mother-in-law. Information, embarrassing and otherwise, was provided by each woman's actual son-in-law.

Premiered: December 4, 1967.

Host: Wink Martindale.

—www.gameshowfame.com

Miscellany

Scaredy Cat

Pentheraphobia is the fear of mothers-in-law. Really. Look it up yourself.

Happy Mother-in-Law Day?

Mother-in-Law Day is the fourth Sunday of October. Every year. Year after year. No lie. In 1981, the House voted 305 to 66 to establish Mother-in-Law Day—your government hard at work.

Monstera Deliciosa

There is a popular houseplant called Mother-in-Law's Tongue. Really, there is! Its scientific name is *Sansevieria trifasciata,* although we've also seen it referred to as *Monstera deliciosa.* The plant has several common names, including Dumb Cane, Dumb Plant, and Snake Plant. And you thought this book wouldn't be educational.

Mother-in-Law's Tongue is native to South America and has several characteristics similar to Skunk Cabbage. The most interesting among them? When either plant is bruised it gives off a skunk-like odor. Also, if you eat Mother-in-Law's Tongue it will paralyze your mouth, tongue, and lips, preventing you from speaking and causing excessive drooling. Lovely!

CHAPTER SEVEN

---◇◇◇---

Wrap-Up

*Unless one pretends to be
stupid and deaf, it is difficult
to be a mother-in-law . . .*
—Chinese proverb

*Of all the peoples whom I have
studied, from city dwellers to cliff
dwellers, I always find that at least
50 percent would prefer to have at
least one jungle between themselves
and their mothers-in-law.*
—attributed to Margaret Mead

$\mathcal{N}$ot all mothers-in-law are necessarily MILDEWs. However, "mother-in-law problems" or what we now refer to as MILDEW, has been around for centuries. As a part of the MILDEW community we've discovered that adding humor to our situations can be a healthy outlet. Can you imagine what the alternatives might be? C'mon, it's funny. Be honest. And we're not above admitting that at times our humor is one-sided. We've never been ashamed of our immaturity when it comes to MILDEW.

What has surprised us is the depth of emotion surrounding MILDEW. Whenever we've received an angry letter or nasty flame (keep reading if you're unfamiliar with the term "flame"), we realize that we've struck a nerve—and then we giggle. You see, the indignant responses are a dead giveaway—the sender is immediately suspected of MILDEW.

When we were collecting stories for this book, we posted several notices on Internet discussion forums worldwide. Thanks to the universal nature of MILDEW, we received a huge response. Sadly, however, one discussion moderator had an unpleasant experience. She received so many flames from the Cyberspace MILDEW Police that she couldn't post any follow-up requests for stories. She shared with us that several of her readers had been offended, although she didn't understand why. Well, *we* know . . . Sounds like MILDEW to us!

What, you may ask, is a flame? Well, it's *not* a fire and it's *definitely not* an old boyfriend. A flame is a rude or derogatory, often passionate, e-mail message aimed at someone else. It can come from anywhere for any rea-

son, but if you've been flamed it's usually because you thought you were being funny or wry, and somebody else thought you were *not* in a big way.* In other words, you touched a nerve.

So we're guessing that there are some worried MILDEWs out there. They may be wondering, "Will my daughter-in-law spill the beans and share a story or two?" Ah, not to worry. Even if she does, we're all just poking a little fun.

---

*Special thanks to Keith Gillespie, Client Enthusiasm Officer (CEO), Client Help Desk, a division of QLM Marketing

Mildew Cleanup

*fter reading this book, you may wonder: Is there a way to change the meaning of MILDEW's "W" from Wrong to Wonderful? Can you turn that frown upside down?

Well, we don't claim to have all the answers, or even most of them. *Mothers-In-Law Do Everything Wrong (**MILDEW**)* is not a self-help book, not a therapy substitute, and definitely not meant to be vindictive. In fact, it's just not meant to be serious. It's meant to be *funny*! It is our dream that MILDEW sufferers (and others) giggle and nod knowingly as they read, muttering "mmm-hmmm" and thinking to themselves, "Wow! I am not alone."

Whether you have wonderful or less-than-wonderful in-laws, most everyone can appreciate a little in-law humor. MILDEW seems to be a universal experience, transcending age, culture, economic status, and geography. Our story contributors range in age from twenty to seventy. We received stories from across the United States as well as from Mexico, India, Australia, Canada, and the United Kingdom. We've got all creeds and cultures, ranging from Jewish to Catholic to Muslim and from Irish to Italian to Korean and more. MIL-DEW also transcends time, with stories documented from as far back as the first and second centuries!

MILDEW used to get us aggravated, sometimes frustrated, and frequently left us incredulous and amazed. Okay, to be honest, sometimes we still experience all that and more. But overall we've become more philosophical. In the same vein as *Wall Street*'s Gordon Gekko, who said, "Greed is good," we say, "Humor is good." There's no substitute for a good giggle.

Most of us know that, realistically, there's no true remedy for MILDEW. Even with a self-help book we realize, deep down, that our mothers-in-law are not going to change. So why not turn lemons into lemonade? Humor is a universal antidote. So wipe that MILDEW away!

Here's a suggestion: Keep paper and pen handy for MIL-DEW's next visit. You can take notes for future story confabs with your friends. Or you can contribute to our next book. Regardless, you'll find it empowering. You may even surprise yourself by feeling disappointed if MILDEW doesn't say anything "blooper" worthy.

If you've got some stories you'd like to share, you can e-mail them to us at stories@mymildew.com. Save your mean and hurtful stories for your therapists; we'll take the funny ones. No flames, please. In fact, you should visit our Web site at www.mymildew.com.

About Our Pseudonyms

*W*e have to let you in on a little joke. At first glance you may think that we chose our pseudonyms at random. *Au contraire!* Our first names are our real middle names, and our last names are a play-on-words based on our maiden names.

So if you ever find yourself needing to disguise your identity, feel free to use our top-secret formula, or some variation, for your very own alter-ego.

Inquiries concerning rights should be addressed to:
William Morris Agency, Inc.
1325 Avenue of the Americas
New York, NY 10019
Attn: Biff Liff

First performed at the Alvin Theatre in
New York City, NY, on November 25, 1959.